THE UNFU*KWITHABLE
LIFE

---

7 Codes to Embrace Connection and Vulnerability
to Create a Life of Inspiration and Freedom

AMBER HAWKEN

To Mum, thank you for being everything you were and everything you weren't.

You're perfect, and I love you.

CONTENTS

PREFACE 1

THE 7 CODES 29

CODE ONE...65
BE FEARLESSLY AUTHENTIC

CODE TWO...128
LOVE AND ACCEPT YOURSELF UNCONDITIONALLY

CODE THREE..161
LEAD WITH YOUR HEART, GUIDE WITH YOUR HEAD

CODE FOUR 183
GET CONNECTED

CODE FIVE..207
FEEL IT, FREE IT

CODE SIX..238
NURTURE YOUR WILD SIDE

CODE SEVEN 267
CHOOSE LOVE

REFERENCES 287

FREE TO SHINE

HOW BEING UNFUCKWITHABLE MAKES US CARE AND CONTRIBUTE

Free to Shine is an NGO that you contributed to when you purchased this book.

Did you know that a sex trafficking victim is often raped 10-20 times a day, so in a period of 6 months that's anywhere between 1,800 to 3,600 times?

What about the fact that at around 20 years of age, after a lifetime of her body being purchased at the price of a cup of coffee, she is simply released, for she is no longer fresh and thus deemed useless in the trafficking industry?

How about the fact that whenever a girl is rescued from sex trafficking, that another is plucked from for her life to replace her, and that rescuing while a miracle in itself, doesn't end the problem?

Would you believe that when asked what it is that they needed most, girls who have been trafficked simply said, "To prevent it happening to anyone else"?

Out of all the 100's of organisations in Cambodia, none of them at this point, focus on prevention alone in a systemised, focused way. Except, **Free To Shine**.

Free To Shine is a child protection organisation preventing children from being trafficked into the commercial sex industry, in Cambodia. Free To Shine partner with families and communities to keep their children safe. They work with the police, commune and village leaders, councils for women and children, teacher, and school directors. They secure girls' safety by helping them achieve their rights to access education, safe drinking water, enough food, and adequate shelter.

Nicky Mih is an everyday hero. I sat with this woman and asked her how and why she started Free To shine. I clung to every word as my heart exploded with gratitude for everything that she has worked for. Free To Shine is an organisation that Nicky built from the bottom up; a truly remarkable feat.

AWARENESS: Why It Matters To Me

The journey of an unfuckwithable life is one of awareness and connection.

Sex trafficking is something that the western world currently has little awareness around. We can learn a great deal from realising that right now an estimated 4.5 million people are victims of sex trafficking. While in the western world, we are paralysed by fear and anxiety of failure and rejection.

When all that you want is to stop being raped and find something to eat, leaving a job that makes you miserable or telling the person who you like that you like them seem inconsequential. I know that this is a harsh statement that will make many uncomfortable. I also acknowledge that emotional stress is relative and my intention isn't to disregard the challenges we face in our own worlds. I simply wish to bring attention to the fact that perhaps our hardships have more to do with how we choose to look at life rather than how life actually is. Perspective and awareness are everything.

When we don't know what we don't know, we are powerless in making a change for the better. Be it in our lives or the world itself.

This exact sentence is woven into the pages ahead, referencing our lack of awareness around addiction to short term stimulation, sucking our souls of love and fulfilment. I feel that it parallels with our blindness to the very real and devastating enormity of sex trafficking happening right now. This is why I placed it at the beginning of the book. I wanted to let you know that you are contributing to its prevention, just by having it in your hot little hands.

Every one of these books purchased puts one girl into school for a day, every 250 books builds a house and every 2120 books secure an entire village all preventing children from being trafficked into the commercial sex industry, in Cambodia. Thank you so much.

If someone gave this book to you or you illegally downloaded it (look, it's a reality in today's world), you can head to www.freetoshine.org/donate and donate the cost of this book if you'd like to contribute.

When we give, we always have enough, and the unfuckwithable life is about that; fulfilment form the inside out.

We are so blessed in the western world, spoiled in fact. Numbed from any sense of discomfort with our fancy expensive filtered water, organic freshly pressed almond milk lattes and air-conditioning to escape even the slightest temperate change. We pay thousands of dollars; the price to secure a village from sex trafficking; for a label on a branded piece of clothing.

Now imagine what it would be like, not even having a say in who undresses and touches your body for someone else's pleasure, all day every day?

Head to the website and help these girls claim back the most basic rights to their body and life.

www.freetoshine.org/donate

Lots and lots of love,

Ambz

ACKNOWLEDGMENTS

To every client who I have had the honour of working with; you give my life so much meaning and my work purpose. Your battles, vulnerability, strength, bravery, and dedication to yourself are what built and inspired the words of this book.

Lauren and Ellen, your reflections and transformation have inspired me beyond words.

Dad, thank you for the depth of belief you have always had in my ability to do anything. I absolutely would not be where I am today if not for you. I played it cool for about 27 years, and now the cat is out of the bag, I was always terrified. Your love guided me, and I know that you don't have a clue just how much. This book should be able to give you an idea.

Shazz, thank you for loving, caring for, and sticking by Dad through the toughest conditions. I will forever be grateful beyond words. We all know that you are why he is still breathing today.

Grammy, thank you for the unconditional love that you showed me when I was an angry brat. Because of this, my insatiable desire to expand rapidly could have been (even more of) a catastrophe directed towards all the wrong places. Thank you!

Eddy, my most annoying, the loudest, and most dedicated cheerleader, second only to my Dad, you can take well due credit for this work. You will never know the depths of my gratitude and love for you and our friendship. You have shaped my world and the work that I do each day. You will forever be a shining light in my world, and your unwavering support has always preceded my success.

Rons, thank you for your questions that stimulate next level growth and force me to be the conductor instead of the band. I love you for all the discomfort you stir in me and, of course, our next level conversations that constantly push me beyond current realities.

Alex, your unwavering belief in my message, made this book a reality.

To Rolex, my furry little friend, who raised me from many a slumber when I didn't think that I could face the last legs of this journey alone.

Kurt, Cat, and Beanie, thank you for leading me out of the matrix of my mind and into my body, feelings, and spirit, the hardest and most profound jungle journey that I am still making my way through.

Jo, thank you for always being there, no matter what. Your support has created safety and love in my heart and gives me freedom that I didn't realise existed until you came along.

Daniel, thank you for the thousands of words exchanged that kept me laughing, mischievous, and, most of all, writing, even when I was well beyond exhausted and my side of the world was asleep.

Jill, thank you for the best GIF exchange ever. Your giant heart of compassion and exquisite humour in between this roller coaster was a saviour.

Erin, thank you for being next to me in a café in Brisbane almost two and a half years ago. That day allowed me to see what insane possibilities look like in form.

Emily and Dec, thank you for inspiring this piece over excellent coffee; that conversation is where this all began.

To every barista whose coffee stimulated my cells and inspired many binge editing sessions, you are my heroes.

Espen, thank you for being a mirror that allowed me to see where light needed to shine most in my life. You brought a tremendous amount of clarification in my teachings and self-love.

Thank you to the restaurants in Norway (Prana Kafe'), Spain, Thailand, Portugal, France, Australia, Indonesia, United Kingdom, The United States of America, Italy, New Zealand, Fiji, Holland, Sweden, and Denmark where I sat for sometimes more than 12 hours and wrote the pages in this book. You provided an environment so loud that it shut out the world and allowed me to write.

And to my soul, my genius, and my ego. Thank you. We did it. We fought hair, tooth, and nail with each other at times, but we did it. Yay!

FROM THE AUTHOR

Thank you.
Thank you for being you.
Thank you for reading this.
Thank you for believing in yourself enough to take a book into your hands that alludes to your power, unlocked.
Thank you for believing in my work.

I have one final note before we get started. I wanted to let you know that I am on this journey with you. This is my jam because I have been, and can still very much be, a strong headed, over thinking, over doing, self-critical, validation seeking human being.

I am *really* human.

Please don't turn these pages and think, "What Amber is saying is impossible. I will never be unfuckwithable. I'll never be able to just be me without fear," because that is not the message.

The message is to practice taking every moment as it comes, good or bad, comfortable and uncomfortable and ride the fucking waves!

Exercise your power of choice to stand in each moment and react by feeling every single part of it. All my feels get going as I write this.

I have never written a book, so I am not sure how open I am supposed to be in this bit. I don't really give a shit, though, because otherwise, what's the point, right?

Does anyone even read this bit? Who knows.

This journey has been insane. I have spent thousands of hours of research, and two and a half years of intensely diving for light inside myself. In that time I also worked with almost 100 private clients successfully applying the principles of this book.

My mum passed away, and I went around the world three times while writing this book, so you will potentially see a few different versions of Amber amongst the words.

I guess this is what I am trying to say.

Embrace all of yourself and all of life. No one gets out alive guys, so have fun. If you are in pain, choose to use it. You are more powerful than you can imagine and, certainly, more than your mind tries to convince you. A breakup and losing your mum in the same month showed me the truth of that cliché Pinterest quote more than ever.

"Feet, what do I need them for If I have wings to fly."

—**Frida Kahlo**

This book has been an entire layer of my ego shedding away. I can feel a lot more depth, simplicity, and satire seeping from my fingers as I already begin my second and third books. It's a dream of mine that you can feel your potential glow inside your chest as you turn these pages. If that happens at any stage, even in the slightest, I'll be pretty damn chuffed.

REMEMBER: Just Be You.

Finally, a few words falling from my mind as I read through this final edit.

Fall hard for the things you love in life, especially yourself. But do not confuse love for infatuation.

Infatuation is thinking that you need X, to be happy, and love is knowing that X will enhance and expand the happiness that is already within you.

Read books. Write a book, even if you never read it, and no one else reads it.

Create for the sake of creation, not for the sake of saving the world. It is not a weight that you need to carry. Life will work itself out; you just need to do what is yours to do.

Risk the loss of everything because we already have all that we need. Loss of what we thought that we needed teaches us this and sets us free.

Don't get stuck in your pain; nothing lasts, nothing. It evolves and changes and grows, but it never sits still, so stop trying to control everything. It is insanity.

Travel, for fuck's sake. Travel!

Our bubbles of the same culture, routine, friends, work, and mindsets are our greatest cages.

Life is a reflection, and if you are looking at the same people, same city, same workout, day in and out, you will only see yourself partially. Let travel reflect your ability to change and grow in ways that you didn't even know existed.

Look in the mirror and scream, "I FUCKING LOVE YOU!" until every cell in your body believes those words.

There is no other truth, and once you align that universal truth with your body, mind, and emotions, you are limitless.

That's enough from me now. I hope that this inspires you to tap into your greatness, but most of all, I hope that you laugh. I hope that you realise that you aren't alone and that you are so very fucking worthy.

Ambz

THE UNFUCKWITHABLE LIFE

7 Codes to Embrace Connection and Vulnerability to Create a Life of Inspiration and Freedom

Unfuckwithable

adj

1. to be in a state of such self-connection and acceptance that peace, authenticity, joy, and inspiration permeate every aspect of life, and fear cannot stop you.

AMBER HAWKEN

PREFACE

PREVENTION: What's Stopping us from being Unfuckwithable?

What if I told you that the root of all evil was not money? It's also not men or religion. The greatest affliction that plagues this planet isn't pollution or Big Pharma.

It's not even tomatoes. *I fucking hate those things.* *sigh*

No. It is *inauthenticity.*

The antidote is inversely authenticity *accessed through connection.*

We are living in an age of addiction to short-term, instant stimulation and gratification, which is quite literally at our fingertips. This accessibility makes it difficult to change the shit that we don't like about our lives because the stimulation acts as a numbing agent. It distracts us from the discomfort created by being inauthentic. It numbs the uneasiness enough for us to ignore the fact that we do not really know ourselves anymore, and, thus, we do not know what we crave at a deeper level. Alas, we settle for much less than our soul desires.

We look around; most people are doing the same thing, so this insanity is barely questioned. We accept quick-fixes and mistake the Band-Aid solution for happiness, even though it is not all that we are capable of experiencing in life.

Inauthenticity is elicited by a resistance to vulnerability, which gives a louder voice to shame, guilt, blame, and regret about the past, empowers stress and anxiety about the future, and is universally experienced as the fear of not being good enough. This fear is inexplicably intertwined with the human experience the moment we unknowingly mistake ourselves as the mental identity of who we are. When we mistake our thoughts for us, we bring life to the concept of what is known in spiritual texts as the ego. The DNA of the ego is made up of the stories and thoughts going through the brain about the perspectives of the world, the people in it, the self, and how it all relates. Its consistency is made from memories of our experience, the things we've been told, and the things that we have seen and accept as reality. Its heartbeat is our incorrect acceptance that the identity of ourselves is all that we are, and its food is fear and the fear of fear itself. Ego fears that we will stop thinking, and thus, it will no longer exist.

I'm here to say that you are not that mental sense of self. Who are you then? Let me ask you a question to help remind you because we've all known our entire lives; we just forget. We get a little, well, disconnected.

Trying to define who we authentically are is like trying to measure happiness with a ruler. You can't, because it is almost impossible to measure or calculate something that has a) no measuring tool and b) we cannot grip between our fingers.

For the sake of context, let's slap a label on it.

The trouble we often have with realising who we are authentically (myself included: a die-hard lover of stats, facts, and figures) is that our mind gets intimated with the concept of being something that it cannot intellectually process

Before I name this 'authentic us' that I'm alluding to cryptically, I'd like to ask you to do yourself a massive favour: forget every understanding about this word (coming up) that you've learned until right now. That way, we can have a clean slate to ensure that we are all on the same page.

SOUL: The Non Thinking Part of Us

Let's call our authentic self our **soul.**

The connection to our soul is severed when we mistake who we are with our ego. It is this very subtle but paramount differentiation between your identity, the ego, and your soul that can help you lead an unfuckwithable life.

Mistaking ourselves as the false image of the ego is what creates a feeling of lack because the nature of analysis (and the nature of the mind and ego) is a relative comparison, which manifests and is experienced as the universal emotion of fear.

More precisely, the feeling of lack, of not being enough, explains why fear is an inextricable part of being human and something that we cannot escape. More so, we walk beside it, understand it, and play with it since we all have a mind, and we all have fears.

If we are living, breathing humans, we will experience it except when we catch our ego, disconnect from the mind, and connect to our soul by paying attention to what is right in front of us.

These skills are what I aim to teach you throughout this book: awareness and connection.

Fear is what drives us into the inauthentic actions that I have summed up as the 7Fs.

The 7Fs

STIMULATION: Behaviors Indulged Into to Consciously or Unconsciously Numb Discomfort

Warning, heavy use of profanity ahead. (Yes, I can appreciate that you decided to read a book with the word fuck in the title, but *how* I am about to use it may offend some.)

Some years ago, I was on a mission to unravel the matrix of negative body image, emotional eating, and other food-related disorders. I discovered that the same impulse behind destructive behaviors such a binge eating or dieting was also responsible for every other addiction; the cause of each impulse was being disconnected from ourselves.

More and more, research helped me understand how we have become a culture of numbing addicts and not just to the narcotic highs. The book 'Chasing the Scream: The First and last Days of the War on Drugs, by Johann Hari, challenges everything that we know about addiction through hundreds of interviews and studies. He concludes that the drugs alone are only responsible for a tiny percentage of addiction, and the rest is caused by disconnection.

"The opposite of addiction isn't sobriety. It's connection. It's all I can offer. It's all that will help [you] at the end. If you are alone, you cannot escape addiction. If you love, you have a chance. For a hundred years, we have sung war songs about addicts. All along, we should have been singing love songs to them."

While Hari explores community connection with others as the major antidote, my theory in this book expands on that with an, even more, vast supply of connection.

I offer information about a type of connection that can never be taken away, that's everlasting, ever-giving, and ever growing when we learn how to cultivate it. And that is the connection with ourselves.

The word "addiction" is derived from a Latin term for "enslaved by" or "bound to." Generally speaking, the brain registers all pleasures in the same way whether they originate from synthetic drug, a like on Facebook, a work promotion, a kiss, or a chocolate brownie.

The brain and neurotransmission processes are complex and constantly re-theorised, so I won't go into them deeply.

However, what we know for sure through both science and, more relevantly, our personal experience is that these behaviours make us feel something other than the discomfort that we are escaping. (Even if we don't realise that we are trying to escape it.)

It's not necessarily always a 'good' feeling (pleasure from dopamine, oxytocin, etc.), and it's not necessarily a 'bad' feeling. It's not even necessarily anything at all. At their most basic functions, the 7Fs simply numb and distract us from emotional, mental, energetic, physical, or spiritual discomfort.

Eventually, I concluded that trying to replace connection with a pleasure agent is like trying to put a round peg in a square hole. We are creating an emotional black hole by using the 7Fs to compensate for lack of connection.

The danger of numbing is far more significant that we would probably like to admit (because admitting would mean acknowledging that we need to give up our beloved crutches). Here is the ticker; we cannot selectively numb life. Numbing is numbing. When you go to the dentist, they stick a needle in your gum to numb the area before drilling, so you don't feel pain, right? Think about it, it doesn't feel good either, does it? It's just numb. When we numb the bad, we also numb the good. So, if we are always numbing fear through the 7Fs, you can guarantee that you are blocking yourself from boundless depths of fulfilment as well.

Connection leads to authentic living through the bypassing of fear. Authentic living gives us a sense of deep peace, wholeness, love, and fulfilment. It makes us unfuckwithable.

I managed to sum up the major escapism behaviors that we see infiltrating our very own lives in seven terms.

I want to state right now that these behaviors aren't strictly dysfunctional escapism. They only become toxic numbing agents when indulged in to escape discomfort, whether conscious or unconscious.

1. Fame: approval and validation, significance; the desire, need, and want to be important, needed, and approved of
2. Fortune: mixing worth, happiness, and/or success with money
3. Fuck: two naked bodies meeting to forget, including relationships that are co-dependent and have conditions around love
4. Food: need I say more
5. False identities: mistaking ourselves as the ego and its many masks, this includes television as we connect with an imagined world to escape our own
6. Fabricated highs: chemicals specifically used to shift the chemistry in our body and brain (drugs, cigarettes, alcohol, etc.)
7. Fashion: not limited to clothing; it's whatever is in. Whatever is repeatedly shown; familiarity is safety to the ego as it tries to hold onto its identity through control. This

could be body shapes, car brands, television shows, or several other things deemed cool by society's standards.

We use the 7Fs to avoid discomfort. They stimulate us and distract us. Feeling lonely? Pull out Tinder, and swipe right until you get a hit. Type XXX into Google. Had a hard day? Rant on Facebook, and get 5 comments and 20 likes. It'll fix you right up. How about a stressful week at work? No worries, relief is just a light of a ciggy or a glass of Pinot away. You totally deserve poisoning your body, right? Constant happy couple photos got your heart hurtin', Netflix binge to the rescue! Or maybe your business isn't doing so well? No worries, why don't you stay up even later and bury yourself in tasks, or share a motivational Instagram quote about how your hustle game reflects your success as a person. It'll go well next to your filtered Snapchat displaying your $13 organic juice and flash car, #spirituallife. Uh oh, body building comp photos are flooding your Facebook feed. You better hit the gym, or maybe, just down an ice cream that eases the blow of your mental comparison to a dehydrated and undernourished body against your own. Perhaps you realise that this world is becoming faker; not to worry, throw on some mala beads and use essential oils to mask the superficiality. Suspecting your last season iPhone or $20 leggings aren't up to par with Sue Jones? No worries, just ask Siri to order you a new set online; they'll be here in 24 hours. The use of these distractions sends us down a vain path of constantly seeking the next fix, compounding insecurities and fears, and being a major part of the self-fulfilling prophecy of stories that keep our fear alive. These activities distract us, but not for long.

The 7Fs are escapism at its most dysfunctional.

We grow up failing to realise that there is a difference between what we think and who we are. We grow up trying to live according to values and a definition of success that aren't our own because they are what we have seen and repeatedly heard from the moment that we burst forth as a wrinkly prune and took our first breath.

If you are to take anything away from this book, it is this: that impulse that you feel when you try to sit still leads to addictions to the 7Fs. These addictions seem to be completely normal in today's world, but they're making us ever more miserable, and thus, ever more craving and at the beck and call of impulse. All because we forgot who the fuck we were.

While life might 'feel' okay, it may lack depth, authenticity, and fulfilment. We may only know the lust of want and desire instead of a limitless, unconditional, and freeing kind of love.

If you aren't allowing this kind of love through connection, you're limiting yourself. You're half living. More so, you are barely tapping into your potential. And that is the driving force of everything I do. I despise wasted potential. I want you to be so fucking unstoppable through the understanding that even the concept of limitation only exists in the realm of the mind. The mind is a tool, and if used correctly, through discipline, patience, persistence, humility, and compassion, will enable you to go places that the ego will tell you are unreachable.

But first, you need to get uncomfortable. You need to begin to look at discomfort and fear as clues that you are exactly on track.

DISCOMFORT: The Space Between Resistance and Acceptance

Every time you feel uncomfortable and challenged while reading this book, know that it is working for you.

I will be spending the first quarter of this book explaining some central concepts before jumping into the seven codes. This way when we approach the codes, you'll be heading in with a good grasp on all of the terms that I use throughout the rest of the book. "Repetition is the mother of all skills," says Tony Robbins, so you may notice that I will reiterate the same teachings over and over again. This is for two reasons: 1) When you finish the book, I know for sure that you will be doing so with a very clear understanding of what is holding you back and how to move through it and 2) In the future, you can open it up at any point and be reminded of the concepts that are repeated and drip fed throughout the entire thing.

My life consists of weaving words in just the right way; a little cockiness, a little vulnerability, and a load of questions; I seek to dangle your potential in front of you, close but also far enough away to force you to reach out and grab it. And it's in the moment when you choose to reach and push farther than you have ever gone that you discover your potential. It's like a mirage, but one that appears in front of you and exists inside of you, and it is only discovered when you grow the balls to go after it. At times, I will attempt to make you feel so desperately empty about the life that you are living, so you are forced to draw the courage to break through the bullshit stories that are keeping you small. I'm a con artist for your ego. Hence the "unfuckwithable life." The ego thinks, "oh yeah, no one can fuck with me," but in fact, I am here to fuck with your ego. Because to truly be unfuckwithable, you must drop the ego and see yourself for who you are.

Everything I say is filled with love. Come, and eat it up. It will require flexibility and trust.

Bye-bye ego.

Hello, unfuckwithable life.

INTENTION: To Create Space and Push You To Move

My purpose when I write, speak, or coach, is to keep you held in the space of love and connection (so you don't run away) and then push you into discomfort so you can move through it. Nothing in life changes (externally) unless we shift (internally). Have you ever known yourself to change when you felt comfortable? No, of course not. What idiot sits on the beach licking ice-cream with the wind gently blowing in their hair thinking, "I should probably do something about my life right now"? No one. The 7Fs act as a blanket for the suffering that our ego identification cultivates within us at a deep level.

Society's idea of success and happiness is a construct where the problem and the solution are provided from the same source and feed off each other. As Daneial Kahenman points out in *Thinking Fast and Slow*, "A reliable way to make people believe in falsehoods is frequent repetition, because familiarity is not easily distinguished from truth. Authoritarian institutions and marketers have always known this fact."

We have seen the smiling faces of people portraying the 'success' and 'happiness' we crave, with a certain body shape, material possessions, social followings and status, business size, flashy brands, skin color, and monetary gains. We eventually unconsciously accept it as truth. A toxic seed is subconsciously planted into our fertile minds. It tells us, *"what you have right now, what you are doing, what you have achieved, and who you are, are not enough."* Just like that, the ego, our insecurities and stress, depression, and anxieties have a fire that will never stop burning. We must step out of that fire ourselves.

You might be asking, "Why should I give a shit about watching a bit of Netflix and indulging in a couple of wines a week? Why is it so dangerous? C'mon, Ambz; what's wrong if I have a few fun flings?"

What is wrong with it? Nothing, absolutely nothing. And, yet, everything. It is part of the human experience, these unconscious decisions. Our unconscious acts (7Fs) create pain on an emotional and physical level until we realise that they are unconscious. This realisation can incite us to make changes, to make better, more fulfilling, and empowering decisions in life, and to live authentically. The problem isn't so much the act itself. The problem is that when we get the hint from our emotions and our intuition, we don't listen. We keep running; we keep indulging; we keep escaping. We don't exercise discipline, choice, and our power to stop numbing.

COLLECTIVE: It's The Small Stuff That Counts

I'm sure that you've all read the ancient Chinese proverb, *the journey of a thousand miles begins with a single step*, right? Well, imagine if your entire life was made up of small, inauthentic acts. Empty, Tinder sex here, a bucket of ice-cream and wallowing in self-pity there, scrolling Facebook in the car, on the toilet, when you wake up, when you're going to sleep, hanging out with friends who are fun but never around when you need them, sticking around in a job that pays the bills, and drinking most weekends... Individually, they're not exceptionally destructive. But together, they're your life.

These small habits culminate into large, inauthentic chunks. They make up relationships, careers, friendship circles, living arrangements, and most of your entire personality. What if the beliefs about who you are were just things that you heard or told yourself enough times and were a load of rubbish? What if the personality people described you as (funny, fun, shy, powerful, extroverted, introverted, daring, dumb, masculine, feminine) were all just roles that you played? Now they feel so habitual that you cannot tell you've got a layer of inauthentic beliefs confining you. Just something to ponder. We'll explore that later.

There is no blame here. I can guarantee you that not only is this layer of confinement true in my life many times over but also it is a necessary part of all our lives. We are born to shed layers and realise that our ego exists for the pure reason of helping us evolve on a much deeper, soul level. It's our acts of inauthentic living that turn into the hard lessons. We all rise through transformed, like a phoenix from ashes. Shrek was right; we all have layers. And we set off on a journey of a hero, each facing our challenges, tragedies, triumphs, wisdom, and becoming the wiser teacher, ever more each time. Only to wash, rinse, and repeat.

Life is constantly trying to guide us back to ourselves, back to authentic connection, back home. That's how we know that we are always exactly where we need to be. It's just a matter of how bumpy that road is and how much of the journey you're flipping birds to strangers, feeling like the world is your enemy, and how much is fulfilling experiences and feeling a deep sense of love and gratitude moment to moment.

To break free, we must realise that we've wrapped ourselves in a cocoon of our illusions and habits of escape that numb and bring us immediate, but short-lived, relief from disconnection in attempts to feel safe.

LIMITATIONS: The Stories That Feel Real, That Keep Us Stuck

How many people do you hear complaining about major areas of their life while doing jack shit to change them? We feel powerless when we live in an inauthentic manner, but we're unsure about what to do with it. Our inauthentic layers and habits have been there so long that escaping hundreds of times a day becomes your reality and your consolation all at once. The truth is that we were never powerless; we have just been giving away our power by believing these three following things:

- We are *fine.*
- We are powerless
- We have no choice.

The addictive behaviors that we indulge in like overeating, over liking, over tinkering, over posting, over-working, over earning, over shopping, and over-exercising are commonly considered quite normal, and thus, we fall ignorant to our suffering. We don't know what we don't know, until we know it all too well, of course. We aren't aware of their self-imposed suffering until it hits the toxic stage and shows up and only then do we pay attention and vainly fall into the loop of treating the symptom. We chase our fear and our pain instead of chasing the cause, and we end up in a never-ending loop called the human condition, and we have no idea why the pain never goes away.

> "It is a natural human instinct to turn our fears into symbols and destroy the symbols, in the hope that it will destroy the fear. It is a logic that keeps recurring throughout human history, from the Crusades to the witch hunts to the present day."
>
> **—Johann Hari, *Chasing the Scream: The First and Last Days of the War on Drugs***

Feeling insecure must be caused by my body shape; I better go on a diet.

Feeling unlovable must be because of my boob size; I better get implants.

Feeling lonely must be because I am not cool; I better start bagging everyone else out to make myself feel better.

Feeling unworthy so I better over give to everyone around me to make sure that they know I am valuable.

Feeling helpless so I better whine about my problems on Facebook and get some love and attention.

Feeling insignificant so I better get a loan that I can't afford to match the outfit that's more expensive than my monthly grocery bill to make sure people see me as someone who has made it.

We need to stop treating the symptoms and pull the problem out by the root. We need to form a connection with who we are, rather than waste a lifetime building up the projection of who we are not.

We constantly chase symptoms and drive the knife of fear into our soul, cutting the threads between our heart and mind, initiating fear, and driving our impulse to escape discomfort. Slowly but surely, we are breeding ourselves to be addicts to these external numbing agents available to us at every turn. It's so obvious, but we remain so blind. How can we be confused as to why anxiety, depression, drug abuse, prescription medication, obesity, crime rates, and suicide are on the rise when we live in a world that encourages and rewards us to walk around wearing a mask that suffocates our life force of authentic living?

I do think we know. We just don't know what to do. So, start with you. Stop trying to save the fucking world, and start saving you. That *is* saving the world. When you place a candle that is struggling to stay alight against another stronger flame, it can burn more brightly even when separated. Therefore, authenticity is your primary purpose, and everything else is secondary. Just being you is the point of life. You must get that. Letting go of your self-perception that is conducted by an orchestra of fear and conditioning inside your mind is what will make you unfuckwithable.

We don't even realise that we are fucking ourselves over.

Most people prefer to remain ignorant and keep their identity, addictions, problems, and obsession close because they feel safe, not wanting to let go, and even defending their agenda.

But eventually at some point, we get sick of our bullshit and realise that we simply aren't satisfied with the short-term fix; when we've sucked our soul dry from insidious stimulation, we begin to look for alternatives. At some point, we realise that an unfuckwithable, authentic, and fulfilling life takes work, humility, patience, presence, responsibility, and consistency. These are so lacking in today's world where everything is available right here, right now. We have forgotten the need for discomfort in the journey to change. We delegate life, try to skip ahead and get anywhere else but right where we are. We feel entitled, yet we aren't willing to face the music that takes us into the depths of what we are running from and into freedom.

UNKNOWN: We Become Trapped When We Avoid The Unknown

There is a story of a king and a criminal that I once heard. As punishment for stealing, the king offered the criminal two options. The first was hanging and the second was to enter a door, but he would not tell the criminal what was behind it. The criminal chose hanging, and when the noose was around his neck, he asked the king what was behind the door. The king laughed and replied, "It's funny you ask because I offer the same two options to every criminal, yet most choose the noose. Behind that door is your freedom, but most would rather face certain death than face the new and unknown."

We must be willing to move through fear; there is no way around it. We can't disconnect from it because fear is intertwined with our life as a human. So, we must dance with it. Once we realise that fear is always going to be there, we can let it guide us and set us free.

Until that day, nothing will ever change.

Nothing will change until we wake up and realise that we are finally ready to let go, ready to transform, and, most of all, willing to do the work to get there. Only then will we be able to walk away from what once comforted us and begin the journey back home to the place we are connected to our very own self, to the place where there is more love, inspiration, and freedom than there is chocolate in Willy Wonka's factory.

I know this is a little heavy, but it's a good heavy, like Beyoncé's strong glute muscles or the depth of a heart that knows true love. I can assure you that no matter how confused you feel right now or how deep you feel you are into your story, it's quite easily sorted. And if you are already picking up what I am putting down, this book will be a good reminder, a nice pocket bible to return to regularly for moments when you forget who you are and let fear creep in.

Inauthenticity is essentially a battle between our head and our heart when our head exclusively wins.

Allow me to explain.

PURPOSE: A Balance Between Head and Heart

I'm a lover of balance between heart and head. I believe we need both.

When we are all one and not the other, we are subsequently refusing to live fully. Thoughts are a function that give us the ability to recount the past through memory or consider the future through imagination, and when directed consciously, we can use our thoughts to redirect our life exactly where we want it to go.

Our soul has an untamable energy and mission, *telos*, that is here to be expressed.

Telos (ˈtɛlɒs): an ultimate purpose or end.

A good part of our mind is the brain. It includes primitive hard-wiring that we all share, like the biological coding for survival that is responsible for the core needs of being important, being in control and safe, being loved and connected. The brain also includes ideas of change. It believes that new is a potential danger and that familiar is safe. Without these needs and fears, tribes would split apart having no requirements for each other or become stagnant, and the human race itself would risk extinction.

Spiritually speaking, I believe we all have unique learning and teachings to discover and express in this lifetime, which drives us forward to contribute to the world around us. Learning and teaching what is ours to learn and teach allows us to evolve. Collectively and individually, our ultimate purpose is to return to ourselves every single moment, grounding ourselves in who we are, flow through life from that space, and get connected. *Connection allows us to be authentic.*

True fulfilment, the feeling of being full from the inside, can never be achieved through outside means. It is to come home to your values and live them. All else in this world is fickle in comparison to the experience of connection and authentic expression.

Essentially, human needs and spiritual values are often in direct conflict. To be able to express your soul authentically, you risk being considered a social rebel and are vulnerable to rejection and exile from the tribe. Our inbuilt fear of rejection is the automatic function of the ego that has us scampering into conformity. Thus, most people end up living out their lives to fulfill their primitive needs and desires, completely ignoring our deepest purpose. Fear is fear. Its sole purpose is to keep us alive through remaining safe, and it will say whatever it can to keep us in that safety box as highlighted by the following excerpt.

"Once there was a young warrior. Her teacher told her that she had to do battle with fear. She didn't want to do that. It seemed too aggressive; it was scary; it seemed unfriendly. But the teacher said she had to do it and gave her the instructions for the battle. The day arrived. The student warrior stood on one side, and fear stood on the other. The warrior was feeling very small, and fear was looking big and wrathful. They both had their weapons. The young warrior roused herself and went toward fear, prostrated three times, and asked, 'May I have permission to go into battle with you?' Fear said, 'Thank you for showing me so much respect that you ask permission.' Then, the young warrior said, 'How can I defeat you?' Fear replied, 'My weapons are that I talk fast, and I get very close to your face. Then you get completely unnerved, and you do whatever I say. If you don't do what I tell you, I have no power. You can listen to me, and you can have respect for me. You can even be convinced by me. But if you don't do what I say, I have no power.' In that way, the student warrior learned how to defeat fear."

—Pema Chödrön, *When Things Fall Apart: Heart Advice for Difficult Times*

Growth, expansion, and fulfilment are always on the other side of whatever fear tells us is too risky and dangerous. Therefore, fear is our guide, and we must follow it.

Don't hate on fear; it's just doing its job. It's up to us to do ours and simply not to give it attention. Therefore, we let it be without letting it affect our actions. Just like everything in life, once fear is accepted as being there, not fought against or attempted to contain and control, it will have no power over us. It is all about surrender, this unfuckwithable life stuff. Accept, let go, and be unfuckwithable.

AUTHENTICITY: Showing Up Unapologetically and Mindfully Without The Need For Applause

Authenticity is the cure to suffering and the birth of being unfuckwithable.

But what is authenticity exactly? When I talk about authenticity, it encompasses both spiritual and human experiences intertwined. It is the *choice* of honoring both your values and your worth, regardless of your imperfections, by connecting with the fundamental essence that we all share. Deep, right? I kind of love it.

What if I said that it was possible to wake up and not worry about who you need to impress, what you wish you could change about the past, what the future holds for you, or what people think of you? What if we could be free from having to feel in control, be viewed as someone of importance, strength, success, intelligence, desire, or authority? What if being you was enough?

This life feels like the freedom of being you while accepting others for being them no matter what that looks like at any point.

It is the ability to let go of differences and be open to your limitless potential.

There is no jealousy, no competition, and no worry.

It is an honest life where nothing is taken personally.

It is a life where you're unfuckwithable.

This book is about understanding, evolving, releasing, and expressing your true self as you take steps to live authentically. It's for those who want to take what was previously in the 'too fucking hard' basket and question everything to become unfuckwithable.

I'm not suggesting a fearless life. I'm suggesting that understanding that the root of fear is either our primitive hardwiring designed to protect us from physical harm or the root existence of the ego. Using our fear occurs through a connection to your soul and through not allowing the ego to be in charge. Fear shows up wearing all sorts of costumes. It has excuses and justifications and stories about why we should just play it small, why change is too hard, and why it's always someone else's fault when we end up in a situation that we don't like. You can be sure that wherever fear is, it's exactly where you need to go. Because the only thing between you and being unfuckwithable is fear dancing in a set of different costumes that make you turn away from really living. On the other side is what you have always wanted. Fear is our subtle, soul Sherpa guiding us towards the beautiful mountains that discomfort and the ego are always seeking to escape. Fear takes us exactly where we need to go to find our power and freedom.

EXPERIMENT: Play With Life and Make Your Own Conclusions

This book is a collection of the books that I have read, the research that I have done, and the studies on human behavioral psychology, emotional healing, and spiritual philosophy that I have deliberated. It contains what I have learned in the few thousand clients that I have worked with and, most of all, my emotional, mental, physical, and spiritual failures and triumphs.

There is no substitute for experience, and I've realised that the best way to figure out what works for you is just to give it all a crack.

AMBER: A Little About Me

I wanted to introduce myself and share my story right now. It might help to know a little about the workings of the mind and the heart that will be speaking to you for the next few hours.

I am insatiably curious about life.

I am so curious that I have pondered whether my soul chose a family where love, acceptance, and connection were scarce, and pain was projected at breakfast in order for me to become inquisitive, specifically about the origin of suffering, or whether that was just a coincidence. My point is that I have had this interest since I can remember.

I have a deep desire to understand how things work.

I was that annoying, and sometimes arrogant, kid who questioned everything. Why? How? Why? Why? Why? But, what if?

My poor teachers and father.

I was the employee who probed every process for cracks. A daughter, friend, lover, colleague, and distant observer who noticed the subtlest lies that we tell ourselves and advised that fear is a place necessary to dive into, understand, and reconcile. This skill has forever been my super power and my nemesis. The truth challenges us, especially when you've got teenager not yet skilled in the art of subtlety or compassion. As a child, to survive emotionally, I become fiercely independent and guarded, and while these walls have been mostly stripped away, I am still chipping at them. At some point post birth, I adopted a sense of worthiness and deservedness of success and happiness. I asked my Dad about me as a kid for this book, and his response was, *"You felt respectfully entitled to participate within the world however you chose to be a part of it, and you cast away anything that wasn't going to be productive or helpful in any way on your endeavor. You were born with the ability to let go of whatever didn't serve you. Just minutes after you were born, you looked around the room and straight into my eyes. It was if you were pleased that you'd ended up exactly where you planned. From that moment, carpe diem was your philosophy".*

My father, one of the kindest, most compassionate, gentle, humble and loving souls that I have ever had the pleasure of knowing, doesn't take much credit. However, I am certain that nurture had a lot to do with this. Growing up, I never once believed that there was anything out of reach. His deep sense of acceptance and love for me kindled a breeze that eventually grew into the force of a hurricane that now encompasses everything I do. Ironically, in my early twenties, as I explored my femininity, I viewed my father as a very weak man because of his soft nature. I blamed him mercilessly for the emotional pain that I experienced as a child because of the rivalry between my stepmother and me. She is a woman for whom I hold the utmost respect and love for as an adult. However, for over a decade and a half, our interactions were toxic. And so, obsession number one of mine was the seedling planted from this very fertile pain: *human psychology*. You'll discover the details of this resolve later.

By the time that I was 12, I had attended 12 funerals. Three were suicides including my stepfather. These deaths further aroused my interest in the human mind. The other deaths were caused by cancer.

My parents separated when I was three. I was never close to my Mum; the mother/daughter relationship was very much reversed. I was bossy and had high expectations that I know she felt she could never meet. Dad was just 27 when I was born and had help from my Mum's mum, Nanny, to care for my older brother and me while he worked. She was my angel; I connected with her more than anyone in this lifetime except my Dad. She was also one of the nine who I lost to cancer.

My Dad has Crohn's disease. In 1992, the excruciating and debilitating inflammation of his GI was still undiagnosed, and he was incorrectly treated for nearly a decade. When he wasn't welding, he was in bed, red-faced, groaning, and grimacing. Growing up, I watched my 6-foot hero lie sweaty and pale, every day, life fading from him. All this illness and death sparked an angry fire that fueled my second obsession: *human physiology*.

I went on to study Medical Radiation Science and graduated as a Radiation Therapist in 2011. Radiation Therapy is a type of treatment for cancer. By 2013, I had resigned. My resignation was twenty percent because of the attitude and energy of those who I worked with at the hospital. 'Blah' is my description. I felt so suppressed by rules and regulations and had to get out. Fifty percent was because I felt that there must be another way. And the rest was because I realised that hospitals had roofs, and I didn't ever want to stop growing.

Movement and health were an innate part of my being. I represented my local area, and eventually my state, for athletics and soccer from a young age up until my late teens. I gave every sport at school a good crack. My family couldn't afford the yummy packet food from the snack aisle, so I grew up on fruit, veggies, and meat, or organic whole foods I believe marketing calls it now. While studying at university, I worked at Planet Fitness, a gym where I held a position in sales, management, personal training, and group fitness instructing. It was in the gym that I discovered that communication, change, and guiding people about what to do was loads of fun and came very naturally to me.

When I graduated, I continued to work as a personal trainer and worked two full-time jobs in 2012. I was still a Radiation Therapist at Royal Brisbane and Women's Hospital, and I was managing high volume outdoor fitness boot camps for women. In both of these places, I witnessed the noxious self-perception of worth measured through aesthetics that was rifling through society's consciousness. Being positioned as a leader and teacher, I began writing a lot of daily inspiration. This became another puzzle to sink my teeth into. I wanted to unpack the keys to success so I could teach it to these ladies. I was trying to figure out who followed through the 12-week challenges and why they were able to stick with it. What was it about some people who yo-yoed that made them do so? Why did people start with what seemed like unstoppable enthusiasm only to disappear and give up? How could some transform their entire body and still be riddled with self-doubt and insecurities (and sometimes not even realise it)? Most importantly, what did those who effortlessly showed up, got results, and walk away transformed inside and out have that the rest didn't?

These questions led me to probe the human psyche much more comprehensively than ever before, and my curiosities from childhood rumbled deeply, calling me back to study.

What did it mean to be happy?

Where did motivation come from?

Why did emotions feel so uncontrollable?

What made us feel like we are enough?

Who defined what enough was?

How could one achieve such a state?

How could we stay in it?

What influenced its presence?

What was the root of sabotage?

It was then that I began external studies of deep state re-patterning, mindfulness based cognitive behavioral therapy, emotional healing, and neuro-linguistic programming alongside my two full-time jobs.

At the end of my first year working at the hospital, I was asked to present at a radiology conference as a new grad. I presented on the topic titled *The Benefits of Exercise and Nutrition for Cancer Patients*. I won a grant to go present at the national conference. After I had walked off stage the first time, the head of the department congratulated me saying, "Well done, Amber. You're incredible at that. Why didn't you study health or do something in presenting?" His words hit me hard. It took me a few seconds to respond, "Why didn't I study health?"

Wasn't that what I just spent the past four years of my life doing?

Nope.

Not even fucking close, I realised. I think Norway has the most honest label of a hospital, *sykehus*, which directly translates to "sick house" in English.

We weren't in health. We were in *sick care*.

"Thanks. You're right," I answered, and I started planning my exit.

After my research presentation, I become acutely aware of the patients' exercise recommendations to rest. And if you've ever been in a public, Australian hospital and seen the pitiful excuse for food that is served, you'll understand why I sometimes think we're better off serving dirt—at least there might be some minerals that the body could absorb. Don't get me wrong, we are well ahead of third world countries with reactive and emergency treatment, but the processed, plastic-like and sugar ridden meals make my body shiver. I remember treating a ten-year-old boy who had stage IV sarcoma. He had been having radiation, chemo, and regular surgeries since he was six years old. He had to be wheeled in on a gurney because he was paralysed from the waist down. And as we lifted him onto the treatment bed, Maltesters chocolates spilled all over the floor. He had a giant bucket of the chocolates in his bed, which had been a gift from his parents. My gut churned. Knowing what I knew about nutrition, it made me so uncomfortable.

I want to clarify that I have a deep respect for modern medicine and hold no contempt, especially for those working in the field. It's fair to say that if you're in the arena of medicine, it's because you want to help. I also appreciate that this boy's parents were willing to do whatever they could to make their baby happy, and I hold the deepest sense of compassion for anyone who has ever or will ever, have to witness their child go through such circumstances. This tale has nothing to do with my perspective and what is wrong or right, just the journey that pushed me here. I discovered a year later, after the mother reached out to me on Facebook, that this little boy passed away. May his soul return vibrant and free.

I booked three months off to travel South America with some girlfriends just after that presentation. I tasted the wilderness of culture and travel. I witnessed the world outside of Western civilization, and the realisation of my ignorance humbled me. Whether that trip was a seed that showed me it was okay to think differently, or it was a moment to step away from the world and pull myself away from the grips of constant over-analysis, it gave me a very different perspective on life.

It gave me perspective that began a new obsession.

Fulfilment.

I returned in the February of 2013 and resigned in April.

For the last four and a half years, I have traveled the world and studied my way through multiple different courses on human behavioral psychology and spiritual philosophy. I've taught over 1000 people individually, a few thousand in small group workshops, and spoken in front of over 25,000 people, collectively, from a stage. I've taught about how our mind and heart can work together more fluently to find a sense of peace with our past and how to create a deeper connection with who we are and what we want in our life. I've written about, spoken to, and coached on the strategies, tools, and wisdom for over 10,000 hours. Most of all, I have dragged myself through the coals of transformation, been humbly knocked down a hundred times over, and I am getting pretty good at getting back up after shedding another layer.

I am a lover of patterns. I like watching the world fit together and repeat and grow and expand on itself. If I can teach you to ebb and weave with life rather than fight against it by writing down and sharing what I've discovered, I'll be a happy camper.

And so, I have put that all together and created this book.

Stop.

Exhale.

Step into that fire in your belly, and get prepared to burn brightly.

THE 7 CODES

CODE ONE: Be Fearlessly Authentic

Strip back all the dishonest layers of who you thought you were, who you think you need to be, what you think you need to do and say and act like and dress like, and how you think that you need to live.

How to do you do this? Work through shame, anxieties, and self-doubt. Access vulnerability, and, most of all, find an invincible peace within yourself. To be fearlessly authentic is to live congruently with your truest values despite the fear that so naturally resides within our human existence.

CODE TWO: Love and Accept Yourself Unconditionally

End the internal battle that leads you to sabotage and shrink away from your potential. Tap into conscious awareness. Let go of the victim mentality. Let go of blame, guilt, resentment, and fear that is holding you back. Nurture the titanium strength of kindness and compassion. No Jedi mind games with your insecurities, stop sabotaging yourself. Phew. And thus...

CODE THREE: Lead With Your Heart, Guide With Your Head

Build your life from creativity and purpose instead of approaching it with suspicion and agonizing doubt. Instead of fear shutting you down, allow it to light you up. Embrace the age old battle between what we value and what our minds say we should value. Find out what it is that you want to do with your life in each moment, and discover how the bloody hell to find the courage to do it. This code is truly the difference between existence and living. Grind, but flow with grace. And as you do this learn to...

CODE FOUR: Get Connected

Seek connection. And I do not mean your thumb to your phone screen scrolling through Facebook or your hands on a glass of Pinot Grigio. Find a connection to your purpose, connection to your breath, and connection to inspiration, calmness, intuition and life force. Connect to how to be utterly right here right now, living. No planning, no thinking, no over-analysing, just live your life. And when you do think, it will come from a place of love and inspiration not from a place of fear of the past or want for the future. Everything you ever need is in that space and leads to...

CODE FIVE: Feel it, Free it

Detox emotionally, man. Get that build-up of suppressed emotions that are creating noxious environments in your body, disrupting your life, and stimulating an undercurrent of emotional turbulence that has become so familiar that heaviness is normal. Learn how to let it go. Learn how to work with emotions, create a healthy relationship with this very normal human part of us, and discover how to listen to them. Dig up what needs to be released. Be able to express your emotions rather than projecting them or being run by them. And you can also consciously...

CODE SIX: Nurture Your Wild Side

Inject unfuckwithable into your veins. Embrace the how to attitude and mindset of unfuckwithable. Break through old conditioning; bring forth strength and depth into your every day; make unfuckwithable something tangible with action steps and palpable wisdom that you can weave into life.

These seven codes can serve as anchor questions. When you find yourself in a life pickle, you can learn to ask:

Am I just being me right now?

Am I choosing love?

Have I loved and accepted unconditionally?

I wrote this book how I would talk to my best friend. I wanted to write something simple, light, and practical that anyone can read and take inspired action, be it changing the way that they think or changing what they are doing.

I felt there were so many options for people who are already on the search and feel they're connected, but what about people who are still figuring this shit out? Because I know I still am, and probably always will be. I need reminding of who I am and how to return to that place all the time.

CODE SEVEN: Choose Love

Learn to live in a state of awareness of your mind's constant fabricated story about how rejection and failure surround every decision that you make. Figure what the heck *love* is, not the romantic kind but the kind that will make you fall deeply in love with life. Live openly, screw superficial stimulation and short-term fixes. Reveal to yourself your divinity, and revere in the essence that all beings reflect this inherent element of the divine.

Be Unfu*kwithable:
A Course For a Life of Growth and Inspiration

I have taught the insightful contents of this book over the years many times and in many ways. But you are ever evolving and so am I. I have no doubt that by the time this book is published, I'll want to add more and change things. So, once again, I want to reiterate, go and test out these theories yourself. That's the only way that you will discover what works for you. My program, Be Unfuckwithable, is a perfect opportunity to indulge in growth for life. In my program, I go into the teachings of this book in great depth and take you through breakthrough techniques that ensure unfuckwithable becomes something tangible and realistic in the flesh. Head to www.amberhawken. com/bu, and check it out.

However, this book and my program are not the answer to life.

I do believe they hold a truth that we need to face if we are going to get to the bottom of mental, emotional, physical, and spiritual breakdown in our world. This isn't a new truth; it is not something I have suddenly discovered. It is the same truth that has been around for thousands of years. I am simply giving the message a different voice for different audiences.

We are looking for a connection in the pits of emptiness. If we want to 'save the world', we must ultimately start with ourselves. We must begin inside. We must connect back home, where it all begins, and it all ends.

We must connect deeply, compassionately, permanently, and fearlessly with ourselves: through connection.

Ignorance isn't bliss anymore; it's fucking destructive. We need to get our heads out of the sand and begin to drink from that fountain of infinite life that lies dormant within us all.

These codes and lessons have enabled me to live with far less fear, self-doubt, insecurities, and the risk of 'ah, fuck!' moments that previously held me back. My intention is that it does the same for you.

Also, if you are a teacher, or corporate influence of any kind, and want to make a difference through introducing this philosophy of connection and authenticity in your educational environment or workplace and help cultivate fulfilment at the deepest level, please reach out to me at hello@amberhawken.com

I intend to create a PG version of these codes for use in school systems and the corporate world to help reduce depression, anxiety, addictions, bullying, body image issues, stress, dis-ease, anxiety, etc. and help cultivate emotional, mental, physical and spiritual empowerment and wellbeing. Most of all, I hope to prevent people from choosing a life that they do not truly love and instead, engage in all they do with inspiration and purpose.

I spend most of my time helping people reverse the disempowering conditions that they learned growing up.

The sooner that we can unravel our limits and engrain empowerment into work environments and education systems, the sooner we will create a more fulfilled, connected, and at peace society, culture, and world.

WHY: Why Would One Want to Be Unfuckwithable?

I'm here to be a purposeful antagonist that makes you rethink life. Why do we need authenticity? Why do I need to address my insecurities? And why does living in the way that I recommend matter?

Chemistry.

> *"Chemistry is the study of change. Elements combine and change into compounds. That's all of life, right? Solution. Dissolution. Growth. Decay. Transformation."*
>
> **—Walter White, *Breaking Bad***

An unfuckwithable life is a commitment to personal alchemy. It is a commitment never to stop growing and evolving, to remain strong yet vulnerable, confident but cautious, and worthy yet humble.

I have a philosophy that I teach in my coaching and my online program, Be Unfuckwithable, which you can find at amber-hawken.com/bu, and it goes like this:

Dig. Discover. Dream. Decide. Do. Repeat.

It means going from not knowing what you don't know, to knowing what you don't know, to mastering what you once didn't know, to expanding your potential and horizons, to expressing your new potential through everything that you are and everything that you do, to actively making changes in your external life, to creating a life that's fulfilling and meaningful; repeat.

Instead, most people usually just do this:

Want more from life, consider changing, try to change things from the outside in. They eventually feel even emptier and get overwhelmed. The belief that they aren't good enough and can't do anything about it is reinforced. Instead of repeating the process of positive growth, this cycle is repeated.

Let's not make that second one you, hey?

CLARITY: Seeing Beyond What The Mind Is Convinced Is True

Our minds can be like a bowl of M&M's at a birthday party. Every time someone reaches for a crisp, delicious chocolate, they leave behind a bit of themselves. Each time we listen to someone, a little of their beliefs are left rattling in our brain. Unwashed hands can spread disease, so can unwashed words. Remember Chinese whispers at school? How does, "Henry loves cats but doesn't like dogs" (not that this would ever be a real sentence because who would like cats and not dogs) turn into "Miss Smith has a crush on Blake"?

PERCEPTION: The More You Know, The Less You *Know*

The conditions of your mind are pervasive, and each has its meaning assigned to its labels and its labels assigned to things in this world. We see life through a unique individual lens and this is something we so often forget. It gets us into strife more than most realise; each argument with someone is a perception clash. Both think they are correct, because in their reality they are.

"The outer world is a reflection of the inner world. Other people's perception of you is a reflection of them; your response to them is an awareness of you."

—Roy T.Bennett, *The Light in the Heart*

The British philosopher, Alan Watts, said, "The menu is not the meal", which I felt fit in my previously stated descriptions of some of the most ambiguous terms in the English language. We can try to describe something that we cannot hold, but every time someone new describes it, it's a little more tainted by his or her perceptions of the world.

Thus, through the many teachings and interpretations, the importance of the message can be lost, diluted, and misunderstood, and now, not taken seriously.

Our individual community and social constructs heavily influence our interpretation and beliefs around words and their meanings. Ultimately, these constructs regulate what we feel safe and comfortable with.

For example, when I ask people what they feel when I say the word money, 80% have an instant negative or shrinking reaction. Personally, if someone says the word god, I feel trapped. The idea that if I don't do things a certain way in life, then I will be punished when I die was so drilled into me that I still have a negative reaction to the word god.

Neither of these words mean the beliefs that our minds have assigned to them, yet that's what we experience because that's what we were told or told ourselves. Remember, our brains are built to oppose unknown territory, so if it senses too much uncertainty or past pain, it will probably trigger uneasiness. Sometimes, we need to look past the primitive impulses because our mind cannot tell the difference between an unfamiliar word and an unfamiliar shadow movement in an alleyway; both trigger caution in our gut.

I'll attempt to simplify some of the most ancient principles around spirituality, including the word itself so that you can realise they're simply very basic practices. Not just half shaved heads, Mala beads, Om tattoos, and excessive yoga pant collections.

While these are my simple breakdowns, I still urge you to continue to decide what feels right for you. And as Deepak says, "Don't follow someone else's map. You should glean teachings from all directions, keeping true to those that bring progress yet remaining open to changes in yourself.".

Here are some of the major buzz words that I feel get thrown around and that I refer to in this book. Remember, these are my (most unbiased as possible) interpretations. Don't flip your lid if you feel that I am left of your field. Just flow with it for a bit.

EGO: Our Collective Thoughts and Filters, Who We Think We Are, and How it Relates to the World

Simply put, the ego is your perception of self that you use to encapsulate your identity; it is your "me" or your "who I am?" The ego is constructed of thoughts that influence how we see ourselves and how we interpret the world around us. Our self-perception begins in early childhood and is influenced by our upbringing, experience, and interactions. Each person's ego is built from their unique influences and experiences.

On top of that, each culture, gender, religion, government, and any other group also has an ego or a set of beliefs and self-perceptions, which also get intertwined amongst the individual ones.

The term ego needs to be understood before we move on any further. Understanding the ego and its role will help make you unfuckwithable and authentic. Understanding the ego will help you pull apart your true identity from your self-perception.

Our human brain has a primitive survival function that continuously interprets information perceived through the five senses. This interpretation gives us the perception of form, the dense, physical experience of life. As Dr. Bruce Lipton so eloquently enlightens us, "When you break everything down to the smallest quantum level, we are spinning vortices of energy. Our physical body, as well as everything else in this world, is composed of energy, all spinning at different speeds, reflecting light at different angles, and creating different colours and densities." The physical experience of life and all the memories, which are simply information interpreted and stored in the brain, becomes a matrix of the mind. The utmost first and last steps to being unfuckwithable are to realise that this matrix of life is the incredibly powerful brain calculating energy spinning at different speeds and translating it as physical objects through our five senses.

Our interpretations are as real to us as the things that we see, smell, touch, taste, and hear. But beyond what the mind can interpret, there is so much more, and that's what we need to pay more attention to. That's what this entire book is about—paying attention to what's beyond thinking, beliefs, perceptions, and interpretations and reconnecting with ourselves.

Our brain has evolved over millions of years, and one of its major jobs is to identify anything that could threaten our life. Emotional and mental discomfort or pain are rationalised by the brain as bad, and this results in many people's lives going down the path of least resistance, one that is safe, easy, comfortable, and familiar.

Ah, fuck. Did I just simply say we play it safe? It's almost insulting to think that people are wasting their lives away because of the false perception of themselves based on an organ seeking to stay alive.

Therefore, most of us will do more to avoid pain than gain pleasure. It's easier and makes sense, right? Wrong.

That is not living. That's surviving.

In his TED talk in 2011, Dr. Ali Binazir stated that it is a 1 in 400 trillion chance that you are alive, basically a fucking miracle. Have you ever asked for a miracle? Well, now you found one. It's you.

Nothing is ever good or bad until two things happen. First, our brain interprets it and labels it good or bad. Second, we believe this conclusion of the mind.

What's the difference between brain, mind, and ego?

Brain: An organ that fires electrical impulses to transport information throughout itself and back into the body via our nervous system. It acts as the coordinating centre of sensation and intellectual and nervous activity.

Mind: An umbrella term that encompasses both the physical brain, the labeled concept of the ego, thinking, feelings, and, at times, intuitive messages and imagination.

Ego: The concept that describes a human identifying with—which means to mistakenly believe that all you are—the swirling, never-ending, repetitive assumptions perceptions of the world and self, separate to everything else based on the five senses. The ego emerges from fear, driven by the primitive survival function of the brain to avoid pain of any kind at all costs.

We could say that you aren't the voice in your head. To avoid being *identified* with the ego, we must observe it and not allow it to drive us.

The ego's life force is thinking, and thus, it will always have stories that keep us analysing, comparing, and resisting anything new or unknown.

In life, that looks like believing the negative stories about ourselves, believing that we are never good enough. It looks like judgment and comparison of others, and conditioning causing us to the mistake of running towards external pleasure and validation as we seek happiness and fulfilment. It keeps us trapped in a world of illusion and habit; it projects values of society and internal mental and emotional suffering as we become trapped in our heads with a constant fearful dialogue about ourselves and the world around us. Fear is an inevitable part of human existence and necessary to function as a human being, but living into it holds us back from evolving and expressing ourselves as a soul.

The victim mentality is the primary toxic resting state of the ego. It is effortless to listen to the repetitive tape of the mind, as opposed to tearing our attention away from negativity and bringing it back to the life in front of us. Our present moment is the only moment that exists, and it is at odds with the imagined version of everything that has gone or could go wrong in life. This negativity is a heavy weight that most people hold, and it makes them very fuckwithable.

They incorrectly assume that there is nothing that they can do to change how they feel or change the circumstances of life because the stories of the ego are excuses. Excuses keeping them stuck because growth, owning our greatness, and taking responsibility is an effort. We must let go of our self-perceptions and own our authenticity in an unknown and limitless space beyond thinking. Therefore, people are afraid to let go of pain, and they avoid taking responsibility. Many would prefer to stay stuck because, deep in their mind, they have a belief that says, "it's dangerous out there without limits and excuses; we cannot control our potential. Let's just stay stuck here in safety instead."

I am here to inform you that there is another option.

Thank fuck, right?

This option requires effort from all of our parts. It requires practice and patience and discipline. It also requires you to have a fuck load of fun in your life, to prioritise what you love, and to laugh at the bullshit excuses that hold us trapped in our stories.

Most of all, the first and last step to being unfuckwithable, is dis-identifying with your thoughts. You must recognise that you have a mind; it thinks thoughts constantly, that's it's job! However, there is no reason why one thought it more true than the next. We know that fear based ones feel very real in our body, as our emotions stream through it. Even still, it's quite often that what we feel is due to fearful analysis and thus negative perspective of the mind. The ego is not negative, thoughts are not negative, but the nature of the ego is self-preservation, which ultimately means everything is filtered through a lens of suspicion. When we believe the suspicious thoughts of the ego, we can feel like everything is a potential threat. We can tell if a thought is egoic if the thoughts are defending, criticising, labelling, protecting, judging, or controlling ourself or another. When we don't recognise the egoic thoughts, this endless stream of analysis becomes who we think we are. Consequently, our world is filtered through a lens of fear.

Being a super sci-fi nerd combined with a strong urge to understand life, I always got a little too excited about Star Wars, The

Matrix, and Lord of The Rings reflecting back the presence of the most powerful aspects of our world. The limitless force of life, the illusory matrix of the mind and the manipulative nature of the ring (the ego).

The urge of the ego to want power and control (or really the energy of our primitive desire to live is left to its own device) leads good people, to do bad things, I.e. Darth Vader.

The matrix helps us see how real our mental projections are and, at the same time, how illusory they can be. And the power of the ring, drawing the greed, creating war and destruction both inside people and throughout the world. Sorry, I went total nerd on you there.

My point is, you do not have to believe fearful, doubtful, scrutinising, controlling thoughts. You are not that thinker.

The brain thinks; thoughts happen. You are the one who can listen and watch it mentally happen.

When you get stuck in your head, I want you to think about the power of choice you can always exercise to direct your mind and see it for what it is. With that awareness, come back home to the space between thoughts where imagination, creativity, peace, intuition, and authenticity exist.

REMINDER: When You Forget How to be Unfuckwithable

These codes are like a checklist. Whenever you find yourself in a pickle, you can whip out the first page and ask yourself, "Am I applying the codes?" If you are stuck, you're not doing one or more of them. Come back to the codes. This book is a reminder, a friend when you are in need, an accountability buddy, and an anchor for remembering how to get unstuck.

The thought patterns of the ego are strongly fixated on what is lacking because the natural role of fear is to observe our surroundings and check for danger. The ego needs activity to exist. Like and dislike, attachment, aversion, greed, and hatred are the main overt activities of the ego. It is like pedalling a bicycle; if we go on pedalling, the bicycle continues to move, but if we stop pedalling the bicycle, it will start slowing down and eventually topple over. When we can disconnect, not stop thinking just disconnect from it, we experience freedom from it.

The ego is just untamed fear of self-preservation. I feel that we can even be grateful for the ego. It is attempting to protect us. It is our lack of awareness of its nature that creates havoc inside. It can just be misunderstood as 'bad', because its filtering process manifests as the everyday fears most of us experience. The key is awareness.

"I am not enough," or, "What if I am unloved and rejected?" and even, "I am a fraud. What if I am found out?" are the foundational fears that every other fear is sprouted from. This fearful fixation leads to defensiveness, doubt, insecurities, shame, guilt, and judgment both internally and externally. When we are identified with our mind, it's almost as if we are wearing a pair of glasses filtered with the command, "I must always be speaking, acting, and thinking in ways in which I can become enough." The perception of our self, the ego, always responds from a place of lack, scarcity, and fear (ultimately of death), which keeps us trapped in our suffering.

Due to our ignorance of not practicing awareness and remembering that we are not our mind, our mind has become the basis of human suffering. The ego is an illusion of self. Why does it feel real? Because we have identified with it; we have heard it and listened to it for so long that we didn't realise that it wasn't us.

DEFINITIONS: And Other Important Concepts and Themes

Emotions

Energy in motion, within the body. A very big surge that grabs our attention.

Beliefs that are conscious and subconscious can be triggered by external information coming in—people we meet, things we see, people's behaviors, movies we watch, things we hear— and influence our emotions. They're immediate and usually short lived. They need to be felt to move through our body, rather than resisted and numbed by the 7Fs. Otherwise, they can get all blocked up inside.

When a subconscious belief is triggered by the outside world, we can feel an emotion before we understand it. Subconscious really just means it slides past what we consciously recognise. We can feel anxiety, stress, depression, and sadness and have no idea where it has come from. Emotions become suppressed when we resist feeling them. We try to control them, box them and often feel shame or guilt about having them. This is just more of the resistance the ego has to being anything but 'perfect'. Feeling emotions requires vulnerability.

Sadness and anger are two of the most core emotions that are suppressed, especially in childhood, and like many childhood behaviors, shape our adult habits. We will often either feel it is wrong to be sad and instead we should be strong. Or that it is wrong to be angry and instead we should compose ourselves. When the conscious mind and the unconscious mind oppose each other, we might have something that we want to change or do, but if the meaning of that same thing is perceived as painful to the unconscious mind, locked in with an emotion that was never felt and released, we won't do it. This concept is what we know as sabotage.

Emotions are the glue that hold beliefs in place. If we want to change behavior in our current life, we need to release the emotions that are gluing the unconscious belief that is locking us into the same patterns of sabotage over and over again. This is where the statement rings true for 95% of our behaviour being unconscious.

We can change our behaviors and reactivity if we shift our beliefs and release the emotions. The entire **Feel it, and Free it** chapter is about understanding how to release this stuff.

Feelings

Feelings are the mental labels that we apply to the experience of an emotion. We can change what we feel by changing our perspective of meaning. This matters because we get to play with our thoughts and change what we feel if we choose. Unfortunately, when we don't take advantage of the mind-body connection, if we always are thinking that we are the thinking, not the seer of the thinking, our feelings tend to feel out of control, and we run, cover, smother, and fear feelings.

Thoughts can change what we feel when we change the perception of the meaning given to an item, person, or an event.

Awareness

Awareness recognises thoughts for thoughts and sees the process of the mind happening externally rather than the mind as me. It's vague because as soon as it's labeled, the concept of awareness becomes a thought rather the awareness itself. You can't label something and keep its essence.

As Einstein said, "It would be possible to describe everything scientifically, but it would make no sense; it would be without meaning as if you described a Beethoven as a variation of wave pressure."

Connection/Presence

Presence, or connection, is non-thinking resulting in being reunited with your awareness.

Fear

Fear is both primitive and learned resistance to change and discomfort. Its only power is holding us back from experiencing love, fulfilment, inspiration, and all those gooey feelings. Fear lies within; it has the cunning ability to convince us that it speaks truth 100% of the time when really, its warnings are useful about 1% of the time. When there is a wild animal chasing us, a cliff edge that we need to be careful of, or a shadow in an alleyway, fear is helpful. In such cases, it correctly instructs us to take care, or it triggers our body to produce an enormous amount of energy and power to enable us to fight or run from a predator.

Most predators that our mind tells us to shy away from are completely harmless, such as past mistakes, failures, perceived imperfections, or perceived rejection. It's up to us to choose to see that it's a sham. Re-read the previous sentence. Unless you understand that part, the rest of the book is futile. You are the one who has to take back your power right now by realising that you get to choose.

Most of the time, your mind over-prepares you for events that do not happen, which sucks the joy, presence, love, and happiness from your very being. Wouldn't it just be easier if we realised that fear is simultaneously keeping us safe and guiding us towards where we need to go?

Love

I won't pretend that I can explain love in its entirety. From romantic to mathematical, there are so many meanings on so many levels amongst all of the languages spoken on this planet. The love that I refer to is more of an energetic one; an energetic and a limitless force. I probably read more books on this one topic alone trying to describe it in the most correct, simple, and unbiased way, and eventually, I decided to let Einstein do his thing and make sense of the illogical parts of life, and bring the word *love* to life for us:

"There is an extremely powerful force that, so far, science has not found a formal explanation to. It is a force that includes and governs all others, and is even behind any phenomenon operating in the universe and has not yet been identified by us. This universal force is LOVE.

"When scientists looked for a unified theory of the universe they forgot the most powerful unseen force. Love is Light, that enlightens those who give and receive it. Love is gravity because it makes some people feel attracted to others. Love is power, because it multiplies the best we have, and allows humanity not to be extinguished in their blind selfishness. Love unfolds and reveals. For love, we live and die.

"This force explains everything and gives meaning to life. This is the variable that we have ignored for too long, maybe because we are afraid of love because it is the only energy in the universe that man has not learned to drive at will.

To give visibility to love, I made a simple substitution in my most famous equation. If instead of $E = mc^2$, we accept that the energy to heal the world can be obtained through love multiplied by the speed of light squared, we arrive at the conclusion that love is the most powerful force there is, because it has no limits."

When you hear people say, "We are all love," this is why.

Authentic

Authenticity is expressing yourself wholesomely, without hiding faults, flaws, mistakes or mistakenly identifying with your ego all of those thoughts and beliefs in our minds. It is expressing your unique values and purpose through just being you, always exclusive of any need to be seen, heard, or validated.

Spiritual

Spirituality is the practice of being (authentic) you.

Meditation

Meditation is concentration and focus. To focus is to meditate. You can do it anywhere, anytime, anyplace, any moment, doing anything.

Responsibility

Your responsibility is to understand that everything that happens in your life, your conscious and your subconscious mind, plays a role. Using your perceptions, wisdom, mind, and intuition, you can change your life, and it is you who is responsible for doing so. External circumstances are simply a reflection of internal happenings. When you accept each moment for what it is and the role that you play in it, you then can choose how you react and respond, which shapes the next reaction and event in your life. Your destiny is the sum of all your actions and reactions. You are responsible for your destiny based on the choices that you make in each moment about how to react, perceive, and act to external forces.

Choice

Our greatest superpower with which we can change our entire reality is choice. Choice is when we exercise taking responsibility.

Purpose

Your purpose is just to be you, authentically. Being unattached, expressing your uniqueness and individual talent and, through this, organically contributing to the lives of others for the betterment of our world.

Duality

Duality is the opposite of unity, which is the two or more coming together. Our universe exists because of the tension between opposites, hot and cold, life and death, growth and decay, gain and loss, positive and negative, flaw and flawlessness, success and failure. The mind processes the world as information at the rate of the duality of energy. This is what gives the nature of the ego the constant perception of lack. The perception of the mind in an attempt to make sense of the physical world sees two halves instead of a whole. That's why spiritual texts refer to oneness and transcendence of duality being "beyond the mind."

Oneness

The natural state of all things, without interference from the mind, is oneness.

[Essentially, I feel the next three are somewhat the same; however, each contains subtle differences. I've separated them for reiteration's sake more than anything. The ego wants to make these grandeur "achievements" in the future, a mind-made goal, which, of course, successfully keeps us from experiencing consciousness itself.]

Consciousness

To see the duality of life at once is consciousness. It is the realisation that there is no such thing as an accident, simply something that has not yet been understood. It requires trust. Life is either acting or reacting to our choices. Therefore, we know that something great is occurring for you, or something is occurring to eventually bring up what needs to be noticed for you to create good for yourself. Consciousness is not resisting natural impermanence and evolution. It understands that life will correct itself. You can become conscious the moment that you choose to look at something differently, without judgment.

Transcend

To transcend is to see the world beyond how the mind processes it.

Transcendence is the tension of opposites that make up our physical existence, thoughts, and emotions, which allows us to be free of the grip of limited existence through the mind. Eckart Tolle, in *A New Earth*, defines transcending as "going from thinking to being, and therefore seeing," or as, "Simply your natural state of felt oneness with Being."

Enlightenment

Enlightenment is being and accepting 100% where you are and what is happening without any desire to change, adjust, alter, analyse, understand or label whatever is. To be enlightened is to be completely aware, accepting and surrender to life. It can also be instant.

What does it mean to be unfuckwithable?

The term unfuckwithable has been floating around the internet for some time. I found it on urban dictionary and researched it's origin without any luck of discovering the original author. Vishen Lakhiani uses it for a chapter title in his book, The Code of the Extraordinary Mind and noted he also found no clear original author. I thought it was fab and wanted to use it for a bigger force of greatness. I changed the original meaning someone gave this made-up word, as you saw at the beginning, to encompass a philosophy that placed us all at the steering wheel of our happiness rather than at the consequence of the world around us. Here is a little more detail about what it means to be unfuckwithable.

An unfuckwithable life isn't about being tough so that no one can fuck with you.

Being unfuckwithable is about being connected to life and ourselves in a way that we can allow each moment to seep deeply into our cells, our minds, our emotions, and our soul. It's about surrender, vulnerability, grace, and courage. It's about accepting our human conditions with unconditional love and stepping up to the task of spiritual expression by standing in our power.

Emerson said, "Life is a journey, not a destination." It doesn't take a genius to translate that he was telling us to stop focusing on the outcomes and savour all moments as equal along the way.

I believe most of our struggles come from wanting to escape an entire half of our lives. The message of unfuckwithable is not to push through pain or fight fear, but to surrender to it instead; allow it to wash over you. Enjoy it.

Here is the trick to an extraordinary life.

Get incredibly close and incredibly comfortable with being uncomfortable, and await the bliss of what comes after sinking into that space.

We long for pleasure and desire always; we want the pot of gold at the end of the rainbow.

People are running through life and missing everything that makes us truly feel alive.

We are all in a rush but to go where?

Away from discomfort, away from pain, into the millionaire club, the end of the hustle?

To 300K followers, at the end of countless hours of photos edits and hashtags?

To the CEO position at the end of the hours with family and friends sacrificed?

On the cover of Muscle Mania magazine at the end of the diet?

To the holiday at the end of the job?

To the climax at the end of fuck?

We are missing the foreplay of life, **the best fucking bits.**

Anyone who knows great loss understands the value of pure joy because the depth of surrender into discomfort is a direct mirror of the depth of the absolute bliss that we experience following that surrender.

It is the pure essence of peace.

Here is the thing, we need each particle of pain and discomfort to experience every piece of pleasure and freedom.

We are so disconnected from being present to where we are right now to get to an outcome that constitutes only half of the whole.

When we live only for the ups without the downs, we are on a constant spinning wheel of escape that results in a minuscule glint of pleasure compared to the expansive possibility of pure fulfilment.

We are human beings.

We are bright shining souls inside this flesh.

We can have the greatest intentions, the facade of expression, and attempts at embodying enlightenment.

But the truth is, we chose this life to go through the duality of dark and light. So, suck it up, and enjoy every part of it. Only when you accept this fate will you slide easily into freedom.

JUST BE YOU: Your Life Purpose.

Come back to this repeatedly, and you will never get lost.

You might feel scared, confused, and overwhelmed at times. But you can do that in your body; you don't need to run from it.

You will always be where you are meant to be, which means you will always get where you are meant to go. Stop spinning. Nothing in this life that is meant for you can be missed.

We always have a choice, yes. But there are certain aspects at play that we don't quite understand and never really will, and sometimes, it's best to ask life for what you want and just sit back and drop that fucking mic.

Stop struggling.

Opinions and noise in your mind can wreak havoc only if you let them.

Come home to yourself in each moment, and you will never get lost in the suffering of the mind. Come home and experience sadness, heartache, fear, insecurities, doubt, shame, and guilt full on. Let them drop over you, into you, and through you like buckets of water that penetrate your very being, and then, you will know what life is all about.

Once you realise that the purpose of life isn't an end goal, it is, in fact, the being of yourself in each moment. Then you can stop running; you can stop rushing, and you will start doing all those things that you wished you had the courage, the time, the money, and the discipline to do. These are all, of course, excuses wrapped up in fear, holding you back from showing up in life.

Fear won't run you because you no longer run from it.

What we run from controls us; what we accept empowers us.

Once you stop living for the end result, each moment will replace the end goal, and with this surrender, every moment will feel just as mind blowing as that single moment you keep escaping your life to get to.

Your bliss is in the moment.

You are unfuckwithable through presence.

Before we get started, it's important to remember....

CHOICE: The Choice is Always Yours; it is Your Superpower

I want to share a story that probably shaped a large portion of my perspective about challenges in life. As I mentioned above, Dad felt I always had this innate ability to let go and move through, but rest assured, I know how I felt in each situation that I was in, and without this kind of influence, I could have turned out a very different person. Thanks, Dad, and thanks Shaz, for forever reflecting and challenging me. Love you both to bits.

My dad was just 23 when he became a father. He comes across as timid in nature and introverted when you initially meet him.

However, he's very strong, very grounded, and lives with more kindness and compassion than anyone I have ever met, to his detriment at times. Despite being over six foot tall and having a fit build like most men on the tools, he was a gentle giant.

I heard her when I woke up, like most mornings for the better half of a decade; my pregnant step-mum spent 45 minutes drilling my Dad about me. This time it was because I was selfish.

That year I had made regionals for athletics, softball, swimming, and soccer, and it cost the family much more than we could afford.

I started getting ready for school, a little scared to venture into the kitchen for Wheetbix. I knew that Dad had to leave for work soon, though, and it would be worse without him there, so I tried to stick to the wall, as invisible as I could get while I grabbed my breakfast. In a kitchen that was 4x4m, including benches, the stove, and cupboard, there was not a lot of hiding space. My step-mum began yelling at me, and after about 15 minutes of trying to get ready and listening to her yell at both Dad and me, I cracked it and started to yell back. I was always more upset that he was being attacked than being yelled at myself. I didn't usually speak back although I wanted to. I knew any retaliation would be met with an amplified reaction; there was no point. I was in the habit of internalising my emotions. In this case, as soon as I saw an opportunity to leave, I did.

I retreated to my room. I would barely flinch when these daily occurrences repeated themselves in various forms. I most certainly never cried. I daren't show her that it was affecting me so much. But on this occasion, as I ran for my hiding spot in my bedroom cupboard, tears broke the barriers of my eyes when she threatened that the stress of money from my sport would kill my unborn sister. It was a weight that I couldn't bear to hold inside.

Dad came into my room and opened the cupboard door. He crouched down, slumping against the frame to sit next to me. I lifted my puffy eyes with an apology. He handed me a cup of tea—his solution to every problem—and smiled. He said to me, "Darling, people in pain will bring you down. It's your choice whether you let them stop you living your life."

It was in that one sentence that I realised it was not about me. It never was. I had to choose to know this and embrace it every single day for the next five years until I moved out of home at 14.

With the help of my second family, the O'Rourkes, and my tiny local soccer club and local community in country Queensland, I raised enough money in raffle ticket sales and donations to stay on every team that I was selected for in athletics, including soccer, for five consecutive years. My step Mum helped with many of these raffles, and despite the incidences above, there were moments of connection. When I was 13 and 14, I made the Queensland women's soccer team. To me at that time, it was like being selected for the Olympics. In the second year of selection, I was vice-captain. We went on to be the only Queensland team in history to go through the international titles undefeated with no goals against us and to win it against the mighty NSW City—the big cats and favourites each year.

That final match remains one of the greatest moments in my life.

(I should note again how much I love and appreciate my step-mum. We all have times in our lives when we have no idea how to process what is going on, and she gave me the greatest lessons that I am now passing onto you. My parents, Sharon and Ashley Hawken, are two of the strongest and most resilient humans I have ever met, and I love them dearly.)

Choice. We always have one.

EXPECTATIONS: What You Might Expect When You Start Practicing Being Unfuckwithable

So, you know when you watch a movie, and if for some reason, the director or the screenwriter doesn't end it where good trumps evil and you just feel meh? There is a reason for that.

It is knowns as the "Hero's Journey," and it has been theorised that it is structured into our DNA to pull us towards growth.

In his book, *Nobody Wants to Read Your Sh*t*, Steven Pressfield notes, "According to C.G. Jung, the hero's journey is a component of the collective unconscious. Joseph Campbell identified it in the myths and legends of virtually every culture on earth. Jung found it arising spontaneously in the dreams and neuroses of his psychiatric patients. The hero's journey arose, both men speculated, from the accumulated experience of humans over millions of years. The hero's journey is like an operating system (or software in an operating system) that each of us receives at birth, hard-wired into our psyches, to help us navigate our passage through life."

It looks a little something like this.

THE HERO'S JOURNEY: The Cycle of Growth in Life

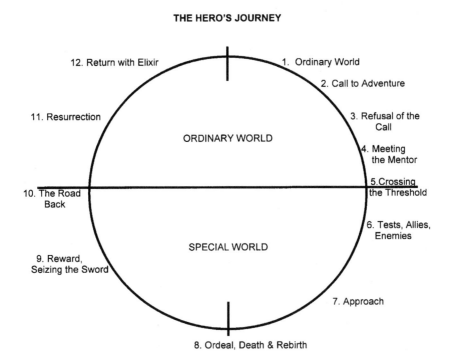

In real life, it reads a little like this.

You have the first couple of steps down pat. You're living life in the ordinary world.

And then you find yourself stuck in a pickle of sorts, as a call for something inconsistent with the ordinary world rings; you're called to an adventure.

At first, you may refuse the call. Well, your mind will at least. You don't want to fix your problem, or you might believe that you can't. Doing so would mean taking responsibility for it, and it wasn't necessarily your fault.

But then, you meet your mentor, whether it's me or another or your own strength within. You might feel some connection with our words or your own courage.

So, you step up and begin to cross the threshold. All this connected chat might just be possible and you read on.

In this book, the enemies you meet will be your very own limits, the ego, fear, confusion, and resistance.

In the hero's journey and in life, you hit some decent road bumps, to say the least. You might even feel so frustrated that you throw down the book in a huff and prove to yourself once again that the freedom and the success you seek are not here or within you. It feels dark in this cave. And then, support arrives. It might be your inspiration within, or potentially, you begin to shift inside, and people start to show up in your life as you work through this book. Whatever we reflect inside gets reflected back to us. You'll notice this as you let go of your limits, incredible beings showing up in your world.

Acquaintances who have been in the wing that you were once blinded to appear. Then, almost suddenly, things go dark, be it in yourself or the life you are living. You're more terrified and at a loss of what to do or where to go next than ever. It seems like there is no end to the darkness, but something happens. A glimmer of light appears. Something in you breaks, and you decide, conscious or not, to find the strength to get through, no matter what. You act despite the odds. You fight your mightiest fight, ready to die (theoretically speaking, you're killing the ego by leaning into fear). And then, the glimmer turns into a key hole. And the keyhole turns into a door. You begin to see your potential coming into form. After a while longer, you begin to see your fucking epic-ness, and you start to believe in yourself. You feel that unwavering trust in yourself and inspiration in your chest. Strength creeps into your every cell, and you are compelled to thrive and keep going.You are ready to shine. You realise what you already knew, and you take this new knowledge and release it out into your life. You create a life of inspiration and success, whatever that looks like for you. You rediscover what you're made of and are inspired to act and share it with those around you.

This entire journey repeats over and over again, each with smaller journeys inside each step.

As Shrek would say, we are like onions, with your soul as the centre and your ego as the layers. And each time our world goes from ordinary to a call to adventure, and we make it all the way through, we've peeled back another ego casing.

The mind is always the greatest enemy we face. Our challenges reflect the level of disconnection that we have with our soul. The more connected we are, the less we resist the calls to adventure, and the faster we move through the layers and return with the elixir.

The only real constant is change, and the only constant of the ego is its resistance to it. The ego works in time because it saves all perceptions of past moments in a memory bank. But the truth is, time isn't real. As it tries to grip onto its self-perception, it holds onto time and tries to control life to create familiarity. Control and static are an impossible mission in a world that is always moving.

Time will weave its stories. And you will regress back to old patterns, and that's okay. It is all a part of it. But through consistent dedication to persistence, truth, and freedom, you will prevail (cue the "Freedom!" scene from Brave Heart into your mind).

After some time, as you continue to commit to the codes, the frequency and intensity of these egoic displays will begin to depreciate. Eventually, your relapse into toxic and self-destructive patterns will be infrequent and a little shocking.

By the way, those crises or relapses can appear in many forms, from wine and chocolate binges to overworking addiction, from adultery to job loss or illness and depression. The shape of the sabotage is irrelevant. It's the duration and intensity that I aim to help you reduce.

Why? Because who the fuck wouldn't want a happier, more stress-free life? So, given that you are human, this is the path that you will tread. This book will leave you with the fail-free skills to be able to go from crisis to transformation with grace, effectiveness, and awareness for the rest of your life.

You'll battle fear and practice love for the rest of your life—that's standard—but you might just be able to lessen the seesaw of polarities that exist in this world.

This book gives you a compass to point you back in the right direction whenever you get disconnected and are lured back into want, desire, and control, whether that want is an unconscious need that rises to feel more awake spiritually or a pair of new killer heels. Both are innocent desires, of course, but the default ego blinds us to what's truly important.

Don't worry! I don't want to take away your killer heels. In fact, I love myself a gorgeous pair of shoes. I simply want to help you retrain your mind in a way so you can enjoy the heels, but you don't *need* the heels.

The difference between wanting and needing is the difference between a free-flowing relationship with life and a life dependent on things external to make you happy. It's not bad to want.

It is, however, a discredit to your magnificence that resides within you to need.

It's vulnerable to admit it, but it's beautiful.

You don't need anything.

You are already whole.

So, without delay, let's get this party started.

BE FEARLESSLY AUTHENTIC

INTRO: Where Authenticity Begins and Ends

When you realise the difference between fear and truth, thinking and knowing, and you and the beliefs in your mind, life begins.

We are all so special. And we are not special at all, not even a little. We are so magnificent that we are insignificant. We are everything, and we are nothing.

"You are not special. You're not a beautiful and unique snowflake. You're the same decaying organic matter as everything else. We're all part of the same compost heap" - Fight Club.

You aren't your personality, characteristics, habits, past actions, or emotions. You're not any label that you place or someone else places on you. You're the original untainted soul you were born as before you became conditioned.

It's that core fear of being rejected and the perception that things are not already whole (enough) that drives inauthenticity.

Our conditions create behaviours that act as armour.

To be authentic, you must alleviate conditions moment to moment, but most of all practice detaching from your thoughts as yourself. Use your mind, yes, but begin to follow a deeper calling. Step into fear; get comfortable with vulnerability until you realise that fear disappears when you don't take it seriously, attach to it, or give it energy.

Fear disappears when you are still enough to sit back and laugh at it rather than be convinced that it's real.

Authenticity is paradoxically a practice, a verb while it is a noun, a description for a state of being.

Being able to express yourself as who you are without the need to be seen, noticed, or accepted is a sure sign of being unfuckwithable.

Before you act, ask yourself, is there an expectation, attachment, or desire for me to get a certain reaction from this action? You'll be shocked at how often you will say yes.

It's only when we lose ourselves that we are free to be anything.

Fear is of the mind.

Authenticity is of the soul.

Therefore, it is fearless to be authentic.

It's an instruction.

It is thoughtless living; it is being.

You lose who you think you needed to be and just become who you already are and have been all along.

Your ego is simply a reflective part of the world that has learned behaviours to escape pain and experience pleasure.

This is an image, these memories, thoughts, and emotions are an integral part of the human experience, designed to allow a soul to evolve, but they are not who you are.

Your evolution, your purpose is to realise this and exist without the reflections.

This type of existence is living authentically.

We can spend every waking moment letting our ego tell us who we are and who we aren't.

Broken or brilliant.

Failure or success.

We can let the past define our destiny, or we can choose it ourselves.

It is your job to invest in practicing letting go of your ego and to begin creating from your soul.

Letting go looks like choosing not to pay attention to these thoughts; let them flow in and flow out. Don't give them attention, don't try to figure it out, just let them be.

To be authentic is to accept and live in a state of presence while paradoxically accepting the human experience of emotions, beliefs, and conditions as a part of life and consciously practicing to rise above them. Being authentic allows you to step into a space of inner peace and freedom. This way, we don't end up reaching for any of the 7Fs and ending up with an empty and shallow life.

Almost all personalities, all personas, all projections and self-perceived ideas about who we think we are makeup layers of illusions.

So, how do you find out who you are? Authenticity is something that you must experience, not figure out mentally.

That part of you that has even a slight desire to be seen for *who you are* is not authentic.

I want to point your attention towards experiencing authenticity rather than describing what it is.

Take a breath and if you like, after you read through this little exercise, close your eyes. This helps you focus because if you are anything like me and love shiny things, you'll be most likely get distracted.

(Obviously, if you are driving, don't close your eyes.)

Pay attention to your eyes for a second, are you squinting?

Is your forehead stretched?

Are your lips pursed?

Is your jaw tense?

Is your throat tight?

Are your shoulders raised?

Can you feel your lungs?

Imagine when you breathe in that your lungs are being filled from the bottom to the top, and when you breathe out, the air is squeezed out from top to bottom. Visualise the oxygen molecules going in and out of your lungs as you breathe in and out.

Now, shift your attention towards your hands.

Find your heart beat. Softly murmur, "Boom, boom, boom" in your mind as it listens to your heart.

Stay there until the heartbeat is louder than your thoughts, which are now just a backdrop, causing no resistance or distraction.

There is a very powerful stillness inside of you that you can feel when you do this. That spot right there, when you weren't thinking about anything, that is authenticity. It's where you can practice authenticity in its purity and, bit by bit, one action at a time, one sentence at a time, one choice to not react to your thoughts at a time, you can nurture this super power and eventually embody it in the functional world. And you can access it anytime. There isn't a single correct or one way to get there. That spot isn't to be confused with an emotion produced by thinking; it's much more subtle than that, I'm sure you felt it. If you didn't, it simply takes time. All you need to do is breathe to get back to this space.

Yes, I see you.

We're in this together.

By the end of this book, you'll get a grip on avoiding distraction. As humans, I expect there will be times that no matter how practiced we are at all of this, we'll lose our shit, emotionally feel overwhelmed and jump back into old patterns. And it's those times when I hope you can flip this baby open and ground yourself in a code t bring yourself back home again, back to authenticity.

I want to warn you. These codes are practices that will require your patience over and over again. While I hope that some of the lessons slap your ego back to 1989 and give you some immediate relief and understanding, it's important for me to emphasise that constant practice of being unfuckwithable is vital. Authenticity is like the emergency condom that sits next to your drawer. You're on your fifth date (or first, no judgment here), and you finally go home with your fresh new partner ready to get a little, ah hem, naked. Up until that moment, the condom has been patiently sitting there, dormant but ready to serve. And then BOOM, things heat up, and suddenly, it's the most valuable tool that you can find. While it might not feel like it's useful all of the time, it will save you when you need it the most.

For those of you who follow me on social media, you may have seen that a few months before I published this book, my mother passed away, I left my long-term relationship, shut down a company, and cancelled my round the world trip to move back to Australia all inside a month. The time following this month was, hands down, one of the most painful times of my life. I was engulfed in loneliness, sadness, grief, heartbreak, and anger, so much that some days, I could barely get out of bed. I didn't want to do life, and it felt as though it would go on forever. I had a fleeting insight into the heaviness that attachment and fear can hold over us when we allow it. Had I not had the tools that I am about to teach you in this book up my sleeve, I daresay that this would not be in your hands right now. They're subtle yet profoundly transformational, and quite frankly, I'm fucking excited to be able to pass them on.

What I'm trying to say is, practice them, and you will be able to move through the darkness of life and access those light moments with much more ease and grace.

***

Authenticity is the gateway to everything you've been looking for in cookie jars, wine bottles, dollar bills, and the approval of the world.

It is the antidote to suffering. The single most vital knowing that any human wants to acquire is that they have a sense of purpose and belonging. We have been lured into finding ourselves in the gym, a Lamborghini, a career title, or a rising Facebook profile, but all that doesn't give happiness. It is well versed on Pinterest that those with less are much happier. A sense of purpose and belonging is found the moment we completely accept ourselves and step into life with courage, bearing our authentic and imperfect selves to the world.

True fulfilment is planted in the seeds of our flaws.

A prerequisite to belonging is wholeness. Let's do the math. If wholeness = 1, then your imperfections are 0.5 and your perfections 0.5. If you only show up with the perfect parts of yourself, do you think you'll feel whole? NO. The western desire for perfection without flaws is the exact thing that creates emptiness and isolation. It fuels the fear of rejection because as we shove our darkness into a box to hide it in an effort show up as "our best selves," our souls feel the desolation of inauthenticity.

Belonging, wholesome, and purpose require us to work and to have the courage to show up, to speak the truth, to not have all the answers, to not have it all together, to fail and be okay with it, to fall apart, empowered and honest, and to be vulnerable, raw, and real.

There is no greater catalyst for courage and inspiration than to be unashamed, to be imperfectly perfect. It requires all of the parts of ourselves to be whole.

You see, authenticity doesn't always feel good. It's normal to feel a little unloved, cast out, and different when you shed layers because everyone else around you is still wearing theirs.

> "When she transformed into a butterfly, the caterpillars spoke not of her beauty but of her weirdness. They wanted her to change back into what she always had been. But she had wings."

—Dean Jackson, *The Poetry of Oneness*

Authenticity from you can make anyone who is being inauthentic feel uncomfortable and challenged. It's not because they're assholes, it's because they're afraid. We are all a little afraid of our greatness and weirdness. We'd rather stay in our heads with criticism, limitations, and excuses than risk being seen. Because, God forbid, we shine a light onto our bullshit and set ourselves free.

Let me explain a little more about the link between authenticity and awareness.

Throughout our lives, we've been conditioned to believe that being true to ourselves matters less than pleasing others, but that is a life unlived if you ask me.

When it comes to authenticity, there is no trying and no pleasing.

Over-compensation and under-compensation are the symptoms for running from your mind-made imperfections. Brene Brown sums these up respectively as "puffing up" or "shrinking."

The perpetrator that breeds this compensatory behaviour is shame. You can recognise a compensator by the way that they project overconfidence. The know it all and are the life of the party. Their social media profile might even be blossoming with infatuated fans. Friends love and adore them and often feel envious of their incredible infectious energy and nature. But anyone vaguely in touch with himself or herself can sniff out the incongruency. It looks like so much effort, and it's often very draining to be around this person. They're always on. But before you judge, pull out compassion. We have all been here. They're deeply ashamed of any part of themselves that isn't on. They also tend to believe their lies, feel they are self-aware and confident, and, sometimes, tether on the narcissist slack line. Their lack of empathy makes them hard to relate to because to be empathetic you need to be able to be vulnerable, which terrifies an over-compensator. Their greatest fear is to look at themselves in a mirror and discover that the image they have upheld is not real. So, they avoid mirrors at all costs, including honest, authentic friendships.

An under-compensator is more subtle. They can be mistaken as introverted but the more obvious sabotage is the feeling of not being good enough. Under-compensating often looks like shying away from compliments, jumping out of the limelight, and fearing to be the centre of attention. Any recognition is met with trepidation and baited breath, feeling positive that someone will see that they are a fraud. Their inner voice often asks them, "Who do you think you are?"

We all have a little bit of both. And clearly, either way, it fucks us over.

Authenticity is the pinnacle of freedom.

Fearless authenticity sounds like a bit of a joke because fear is quite usefully hardwired into our minds. No one wants to be truly fearless; we'd have no sense of self-preservation. To be fearless, we'd need to cut that bit out of our mind, right?

Ah-ha, we're onto something here. The fearless in fearless authenticity isn't the Wonder Woman kind of fearless, even though she's such a hottie. The fearlessness that I'm referring to here is a fearlessness through awareness, AKA non-thought.

Wait for it.

Fearless authenticity implies the non-mind or more accurately beyond the mind. It is not before it, not in it, not through it, but beyond it.

Authenticity *is* effortlessness.

It is non-trying.

It is so fucking simple because it means, in a sense, to stop trying.

But simple does not always mean easy.

Our egos are built on self-promotion whether it be positive or negative, puffing up or shrinking. This means inauthenticity requires more effort, more projection of an identity that is either better than or less than the rest of the world around them at any given moment.

Fearless authenticity is the absence of thought. It stems from a stillness that has neither an agenda nor need to be acknowledged.

In that connected, still space, you discover a freedom that will allow you to break the shackles of who you have been *trying* to be and do to achieve society's material-obsessed definition of happiness.

And the even better news is that fearless authenticity cannot be done wrong as long as you stop *trying* to do it.

Remember our breathing exercise before? Do it again, concentrating of the molecules of air as you inhale and exhale. When you feel peaceful, pick the book up again.

Not a thought ran through your head, did it? This is non-thinking, non-mind. Here, you forget about who you are. You no longer have a name, a lifetime of memories, baggage, or a future of desires and anxieties. You are 100% right where you are, the only place that there ever is. You're in "the now" as Eckhart Tolle calls it. The so-called rise in consciousness simply realises that we are bigger than our mind. Words like "expansive," "invincible," and "the cosmos" are used to describe this experience because that's what it feels like when the mind becomes the background noise rather than the conductor of your life.

So, at this point, you're probably thinking, "Okay, Amber; sure. Great for those few seconds that I was distracted, but now that I'm not and all my problems have returned".

This, my friend, is the voice of the ego. Remember, there is only the now.

Authenticity, as well as meaning non-thinking, equals freedom, vulnerability, connectedness, and consciousness. These are the ideas that we'll be unpacking in this chapter.

Authenticity is not about standing out, protecting your pride, or being seen and heard. That's the opposite of authenticity. We don't want to be in that state of want, but it's also how most people live. The thought that we need to be heard to be important is the ego itself. Being heard is important when it comes to doing what you were born to do on this planet, but doing it should be organic and effortless.

As we shed layers of who we think we are and start to undress the protective, self-defensive, and righteous suits of the ego— naked and magnificent as our real self—we become fearless in our vulnerability.

The ego wants you to be different. Seeking uniqueness is not authenticity.

When our sense of identity is wrapped in or formed by anything outside of ourselves, it's not only limiting but also dangerous. When our entire sense of importance, role, or being is tied into the significance that we receive from the world around us, we act in a way that is inauthentic, always looking for more to satisfy the ego.

Authenticity is the expression of our individual truth while realising that we are squishy bags of flesh with a name and a suited-up soul. Combining fearless authenticity with the titanium strength found from deeper connectedness helps us embrace our magnificence and stop shying away into the fear that keeps our wild hearts trapped in shame. Being fearlessly authentic means being the exact person, soul, and expression who you entered the world as. You knew who you were before all that thinking stuff happened and got in the way of life. There is no need to be anybody else. You have one lifetime to experience yourself as this person. Living in this way sprouts endless opportunity and potential. You have this one life, right now, that you are currently living.

This life is an opportunity for you to realise how important you are as a soul. And just to be you.

Lesson

1 | LET GO: You Are Not Who You *Think* You Are

We all have a way of being that we are here to outgrow.

Maybe who you are being now is not who you really are.

Assume that the more defensive you feel about needing to state, "This is who I am," means the more stuck you are in that fantasy world of "me."

A painful fantasy at that.

It is a fantasy that always has expectations and drains you.

On the surface, this person who you claim to be feels great as the validation streams in by the bucket load from other people praising you.

You know exactly how to play this role and feel very comfortable in being it.

Deep down, though, there is a darkness that stirs. You cover it with tasks, business, and anything you can get your hands on. Sex, food, films, and, most of all, people's approval, which you are always secretly craving.

The truth is that everything has a cycle, including personas. We create many of these throughout our life. Usually, it's the ones that have returned the greatest amount of external love and validation from the world around us that are the most dangerous because we can become addicted to that gratification and love we receive. "Wow, you are so amazing!" "I just love how you (insert behavior X)." These affirmations become our drug of choice.

It's not hard to see why we keep on doing it. The trouble is that all your self-worth is outside of you. You must "be someone" to experience this love and validation. So deep down, you never want to let it go. You defend it to the end, cut the people from your life who challenge this inauthenticity, and sever opportunities that your true self would have seen and been able to receive.

If you fight to protect the image of your current self, your actions, your emotions, your decision making, your communication, and presence, you may never step into who you are.

You might lose out on everything that was coming to you if you were to let go. And all for what? "Being me?"

You are not who you think you are. You are not your beliefs or emotions or actions.

You are what is underneath that.

Until you learn to love the soul inside of you who never receives validation from the world, you'll be living a lie, chasing your tail, and always exhaustingly living up to others expectations of who you need to be or how you feel you need to be perceived.

If you don't let go of who you think you are, you'll never have the opportunity to be who you need to be finally to know that you're enough.

You'll never realise that you didn't need to be anything to anyone—especially not yourself—to be enough.

Give up the show. When you settle for a life of validation and attention from the world around you, you are robbing yourself of the best fucking thing that life has to offer.

Freedom.

The irony is the "you" who defends their "me-ness" is trying to convince you that the act that you play *is* freedom.

"This is just who I am."

Therefore, the only way out is to let go and go within.

You must go deep, deep, deep within.

Within is where you'll discover the love that you crave.

You'll realise that you only feared not being you because in keeping up the façade, you believed the only place where you could find certainty, love, and peace was through the validation outside of yourself.

You could be the only one stopping you from being who you need to be to get where you want to go. What if you are defending greatness and, as a result, sacrificing outstanding? You'll never know if you don't let go.

Here's the secret: it's all inside.

Go there.

Become humble.

Be brave.

And then, you can set yourself free.

Lesson 2
I AM: Ego and "I" Are Just Thoughts

The answer to the question, "Who are you?" is not nearly as definitive or important as answering for yourself, "Who am I?" since that will determine the quality of your very existence.

No pressure!

Okay, you can relax. It's not too hard to work with once you get your head around it. After that, it requires only practice and dedication. If you can handle that, you'll be just fine.

Have you ever noticed how efficient and automatic your mind is? Automatic being the operative word here. That chit-chat is a shared human conditioning layered with thousands of years of programming coupled with your unique set of programs derived from your upbringing and influence. And all together it unconsciously, automatically, directs your life.

The ego loves automatic.

Now, if you're anything like me, with a vivid imagination and varying degrees of understanding of the ego influenced by a bunch of books and blogs that you've read, you may have thought at some point, or even still think, that this ego is some real living alien thing that you need to get rid of.

Well, it's not. The ego isn't evil. It's simply the constant state of lack that we experience because of believing that the ego—all of those fear-based thoughts and beliefs in our minds—is who we are.

Let me be clear. We totally need it! And it's impossible to get rid of it anyway. Plus, it serves an essential role in our personal growth and evolution as a soul.

Recognise any of the following thoughts?

My troubles.
I need to find my purpose.
I feel depressed.
I want someone to love me.
I need to change, but *I* just can't find the motivation.
My life is meaningless.

The problem is not the problem. The problem is the illusion that the chorus of constant want, need, and desire in your head is *you*.

The ego is never satisfied.

The role of the ego is to produce an identity to function and interpret information in this world of form. It is always looking for danger and signs of a threat to your physical safety as well as your emotional safety and self-esteem. It is, therefore, always in fear. That is what it's there for. It also sees the world in duality, an unconscious binary interpretation of every bit of information coming in to be processed, and it gives us a value for each item. In a sense, everything the ego processes is either seen as right or wrong, good or bad, positive or negative. It judges *everything* and accepts nothing *just as it is*. The desire for more positive feelings and the escapism of negative feelings is the natural state of the ego.

When we unconsciously accept every thought in our mind as real, every part of the information processed in duality, we will always be in a constant state of lack. We will feel unfulfilled.

That's why the ego gets a bad rep; it's the self-preserving entity that is never satisfied.

Exercise: Comparison

Open your Instagram account or Facebook account.

Scroll through and notice what the mind says. Is it judging what people are wearing? Is it comparing your life to theirs? Is it belittling you or someone else?

If it is, you know that this is the ego, not you and not reality. An authentic state of being would be feeling inspired and joyous for others, peaceful and calm.

Note: If you don't have social media, you could apply this example to a conversation you are having with someone around his or her achievements and notice what happens inside of you.

What if we saw the ego for what it was, accepted it, and learned to use it? It's going to be there anyway, so we may as well just let it be rather than resist it, right?

Now, we cannot survive without our mind, but we can move *through* it or beyond it.

It's in our desire to be seen that we make ourselves invisible in this world. The belief that being seen and heard is more important than being authentic will alone create destructive darkness in your life.

Take any cliché quote like, "Desire nothing and free yourself from suffering," or, "Want less, be more," or, "Weep with joy in our new-found wisdom." Next minute, we return to the addictive stimulation of our insufferable Pokémon Go. Why? Because it's insane to tell you to simply let go of desire. Like, how the fuck does one let go? We may as well go around saying "Be true to you."

Do you know what you want?

I bet you could tell me what you don't want.

I don't want to be fat

I don't want to be hated.

I don't want to be poor.

I don't want to be alone.

Every *I* has an individual set of beliefs that dictate choice, emotions, and reactions, which essentially determine our entire life and how it is lived. These beliefs dictate what we do and don't do, how we define success, love, happiness, attractiveness, meaning. It determines what job we go for, what we give a shit about and what we don't give a shit about, whom we marry, how pissed off we get in a traffic jam, or how blissful we feel taking a day off and relaxing with friends. The *I* has an entire rule book for what we believe and how we feel about life.

If we stopped for a second, took a moment out of our self-absorbed crusade for happiness, and realised the cause of all of our suffering, we could stop suffering.

Our *I* influences our emotions. We live on a moment-to-moment basis experiencing emotions running through our body. To a large extent, our quality of life is determined by the quality of our emotions.

If we're going to get into the crux of the matter, we must face one simple truth. The *I*, the want for survival, and the search for meaning are hardwired into the existence of our brain. If we entirely got rid of our ego, we'd have no desire to progress, evolve, learn, or thrive.

The entire point of life is to come in as humans, do human things, fuck up, love, fail, desire, and then realise we need to stop doing that; this is called evolution.

If that perception didn't tickle your fancy, maybe you'd prefer to choose to live on the hardwire default, where complaining, worrying, stress, and anxiety are all terribly normal experiences all day, every day. Nope? I thought not. So, why not choose to see life as an adventure, one to be lived with meaning, purpose, perfect moments of imperfection, without the need for judgment or comparison to boost your esteem?

If you stop letting your mind run you, you are free to create whatever meaning and experience that you choose. Hopefully experiences of inspiration and contribution for the better, for the world around you.

The ego exists through words and labels. As you are learning, we are so much more than words, labels, and the ego. When you stop labelling yourself, you stop limiting yourself.

You can be anything that you want to be. So, stop labelling and start living.

You are more than your thoughts.

Exercise: Name your ego.

Personification is a powerful way to recognise when you are being inauthentic. You can spot the ego type patterns and rise above them. So, I suggest giving your ego a name. Something funny is always powerful as humour shatters the ego almost instantly. From that point forward, you can use this as an anchor, to pull yourself out of a negative spiral, judgment, comparisons, fearful state, worry, greed, desire, insecurities, shame, guilt, and anger when they're not serving you because they can, more on this later. By simply realising that it's a story, an attempt from the ego to grow stronger, you can centre yourself.

Note: if you find it hard to let go, just know that that's okay. At first, it will be more challenging to let go of negativity because it's been the fuel of the ego for so long and is wrapped in your sense of self. It gets a lot easier the more you practice.

Lesson 3

SIMPLICITY: Authenticity Lies in Simplicity

Knowing others is intelligence;
knowing yourself is true wisdom.
Mastering others is strength;
mastering yourself is true power.

—Lao Tzu, *Tao Te Ching*

Fearless authenticity is accessed in a state of presence where there is no duality, where we are already whole, where there is nothing to add and nothing to take away.

It's a space where you are stripped of your personal identity. The irony of teaching about being authentic is that there is nothing to be done, only habits to be undone. You are already whole underneath your mind.

The idea is to try less and do less. Instead of giving in to the ever-desiring ego, start to retrain your brain to be still and experience simple, authentic bliss.

You aren't in danger of being an unconscious douche-bag if you have an ego, like most personal development or spiritual teachers elude too. You can be authentic and have an ego at the same time.

Sure, the ego is a never-ending energy-sucking parasite that always wants more, but it is also what keeps us going. The inner need to evolve is what brought you here.

If you were simply satisfied already, you: a) wouldn't need this book, because you'd believe that you'd already figured out the answer to life, or, more likely, b) would be living in a state of delusion and not actually satisfied at all but rather in a yoyo of constant internal and external validation. Eventually, of course, that need for validation would crumble, and you would get so fed up wanting *more* that you would seek out this book or something like it.

> For him who has conquered the mind, his mind is for him
> the best of friends; but for one whose mind is uncon-
> trolled, that very mind acts as the worst of enemies.

—Bhagavad Gita, Chapter 6, v. 6

To be consciously and fearlessly authentic, you have to remember these two ideas:

- Intention matters most
- You can still use your mind and be authentic; awareness sits under thought.

I'll expand on point one first. Have you ever said, "I am depressed," or, "I am lazy," or, "I am happy?" Yeah, me too. Well, we were kind of wrong. Okay, we were totally wrong. Here is why. "I" is identification. We aren't our emotions just as much as we aren't out thoughts. Sometimes, we adopt an emotional state or another verb to describe ourselves. Since thoughts influence emotions, and emotions drive behaviour, depending on what we were before "I", this can change our life, actions, and outcomes dramatically.

I had a bloody ball creating a bunch of different personalities that we all place on like hats. Some are different emotional states, some are other descriptive terms, and some are names commonly used. I also added a little story, or belief, next to each persona to bring to light the little bullshit we often tell ourselves.

My bet is, throughout this little adventure to being unfuckwithable, you'll realise just how many stories we really have.

Finally, the beliefs that I've assigned the personas to are slightly different for everyone. These are just examples.

Note: the ego can take on positive personalities as well. It depends how important, different, or strong the ego is. This is technically narcissism when it's unconscious.

- Satirical Shane: "People don't understand me."
- Anxious Ann: "What I have now is not enough?"
- Fearful Fred: "The world is out to get me."
- Embarrassed Emily: "I'm always screwing up."
- Insecure Ian: "What are they thinking about me right now?"
- Sarcastic Susan (Amber) - "Just being me is boring and humour hides my vulnerabilities."
- Late Larry: "It can wait."
- Shameful Sean: "There is something wrong with me."
- Lazy Larry: "Everything is too hard."
- Exhausted Erin: "There is never enough energy."
- Abundant Aiden: "All I need to do is think abundantly, and I will be abundant."
- Agitated Ashley: "I am uncomfortable in myself right now."
- Awkward Adam: "I'm not really sure what the right thing to do here is."
- Raging Ryan: "I have no control over this situation so I will disturb the world around me to feel in control."
- Spiritual Sally: "This version is better than the standard ego, and it's better than all non-spiritual people."
- Different Dylan: "I'm important because I don't fit in and tell myself that I don't want to be important."
- Hilarious Harriet: "Let me avoid vulnerability with this joke."

- Motivated Matt: "It's not good enough how it is right now so I must change it now."
- Egotistical Evan: "I need the world to acknowledge me so I feel good enough."
- Tired Tom: "I have so much to do."
- Overwhelmed Oley: "It's all too much, and I need to get it all done now."
- Evil Eden: "The world is against me."
- Hating Harry: "They should pay; the world owes me."
- Inspired Ian (ingenuine): "I'm totally on purpose right now."

Personally, I spend a lot of time in Hilarious Harriet and Sarcastic Susan. I'm still working on the whole vulnerability thing.

Some of these egos refer to the physical, such as Exhausted Erin. I wanted to clarify that despite well-researched evidence around fear negatively affecting our health, sometimes it is our body giving us feedback that we should listen to. Here is a little tip on how to tell the difference. A brilliant yoga teacher of mine says something in triangle pose, which is known in the Bikram Yoga series as the "master asana" because of its physical difficulty and the mental strength it requires to surrender into it without a struggle. She says, "If your body needs to rest, then drop out, but if it's your mind that is creating weakness body, stay in." I would check in by imagining that I was as light as a feather, and it would often become easy. If it became easier, I knew that my mind was playing a role and fighting the posture, but if my legs were still buckling, I knew that I needed to rest physically. Listen to your body; it never lies.

It is very important not to use the labelling of these different egos as a way to avoid responsibility. For example, saying, "Oh, it was my anger," as if you couldn't help it, is blaming and not taking responsibility. The idea behind labelling the ego as personalities, behaviours, or characteristics is to help you become aware and take responsibility, not give it away. It would be empowering to say, for example, "I feel angry," or, "that triggers insecurity in me." However, it should not be said, "I am," or, "you made me," or, "that made me."

I also want to introduce to you a concept that I came across when I was trying to explain the ego to a client once, which I have called medicinal ego. It also leads to point number two beautifully. Medicinal ego is when we are aware that we are playing a role, and we engage in it for the purpose of breaking someone's egoic state. Humour is exceptional for this. Consider comedians and how they get away with saying things that are incredibly honest but otherwise could be taken offense to. Humour makes it easier to swallow the truth because it breaks the normal neural pattern and interrupts the normal ego reaction. Humour is the difference between what we expected to happen and what happened.

You might be asking, "So, is every personality ego based and fake?"

No. And there are subtle yet very important differences between someone who is fuckwithable and unfuckwithable, and that is attachment.

Attachment comes with the expectation or desire for a specific reaction from the outside world. As previously mentioned, identity is the strongest force in the human experience. When someone pokes at our personality or challenges our beliefs or does/says something that doesn't align with our reality and we are identified with the ego, we experience the feeling of threat, which is expressed by what we know as taking something personally. When we are attached to our ego, we are attached to expectations, and we easily become irritated with the world around us. We feel frustrated and irritated and just in general crabby. I have a very technical (totally kidding) exercise to measure your ability to let go, surrender, detach, and flow with life, not need to be seen and heard as a certain kind of person, and your ability to let go of states and show appreciation. Let your ego take over for a second with this story, and, thus, return to the world with conscious awareness and authenticity. It's called the Jenga Test.

Exercise: The Jenga Test

This is my favourite exercise that I've ever thought of. Note, I was two wines deep when I made it up, but let's not let that get in the way of transforming our lives, eh?

This test can be used at any time in our life, or maybe even a little inside joke to yourself or between unfuckwithable friends.

Play a game of Jenga, and observe very carefully how you play the game, especially if the tower falls on your go. Do you get annoyed that you lost? Are you irritated and frustrated, and do you lose your shit when the Jenga blocks fall? Or are you simply accepting that the Jenga tower is now in ruins?

Now, relate this to life. Do you rush the building of the tower? Are you conscious or careless in your actions and thoughts? When things don't go your way, how do you react? Do you fall victim to what happens? Do you blame the person before you? Do you fall apart because the world seems to be falling apart or are you able to accept things how they are, without feeding into the ego?

Point number two, expansion:

What I've come to realise after initially thinking, "Oh shit, to be conscious and authentic means I have to be boring as fuck," is that you're not fully disconnected through thinking.

We can watch our ego play out, our beliefs and emotions fly by, and still be present. We can use our mind to direct our experience, to think, to solve problems when we need to, and still be in a state of authenticity.

I decided to experiment and surrender and see where it took me. Through surrender, I could see how much of my behaviour was stemming from my ego's need to be seen and heard. Even in my everyday teaching of authenticity and freedom, I would watch back videos and cringe. I have no doubt that as you begin to let go of who you think you are and observe the never-ending opinions and the reflex need for validation, you'll see how much of who you think you are was just a role that you'd been fitting into smugly for a very long time.

The mind is our most powerful tool, a marvel of creation. Like any other tool, it is subject to being misused. Translation: We aren't so much using the mind in a wrong way. It's that we aren't aware of the difference between us and our mind; therefore, it is playing us like a fiddle, using us. Eckhart Tolle refers to this misuse as "the disease." The disease is when "you believe that you are your mind. This is the delusion."

To be authentic, you can simply be who you are and do what comes naturally. Eventually, you'll figure out what that is. It is that simple. I believe each soul is unique. Once you begin to play with observing your thoughts and not acting, you figure out what that uniqueness is and start to live with fearless authenticity. You learn how to live with a pure intention and zero effort spent on seeking validation. It's such a freeing place; hence, I call it unfuckwithable.

Let me have a guess at how this is going to go for you for a while. At first glance of yourself, when you begin to look deeper, you may start to realise that you're on repeat behaviour on a surface level. You've learned what gets you validation. So, you mimic, and you act to get more of the same. It's fucked up really! Normal, and most people do it, but it's fucked up!

What can we do about that? Well, as Lao Tzu says, "act without expectation."

Just try it.

Put the fears aside for a second. Resist arguing or puffing up. Notice how your self-chatter is either defending or criticising my words or your sense of self. That's what the ego does. It's what it is. But remember, that is not *you*. It's just your ego seeing its death. It doesn't realise that you now know what it is, so it's holding on to survival by the only way it knows how, which is to reject and judge itself or another, to become separate and different.

We might ask then, "Without my thinking mind, am I anyone? Without experiences, thoughts, and emotional attachments, am I anything?"

It's at about this stage that the ego will crack the shits.

"What's the fucking point? Screw that. I'm going back to being whoever I want. You can't tell me to stop being who I am and just be nothing and sit here and think nothing and be useless."

Hold your horses, ego; I'm getting there.

Right about now, the ego will worm its way in and puff up (Inflate and shrink as it compares). It will puff up by denying because denying makes you oh so very important. The more different it can be, the better. The better it can be, the more different it is. Both reactions serve as a way of strengthening the ego. It will *also* shrink by self-criticism because wrong is effectually still different, still separate. This shrinking side of the ego is often referred to as victim mentality. It's where a lot of people spend their energy and time as they seek external and internal validation. And it's a lot easier than the self-righteous side of the ego, but it's exhausting.

It's exhausting even to write it. I bet it's exhausting to read too. How fucking exhausting do you think it is to live it?

What could you do with all that extra energy?

What life could you live?

How would you show up if you had no previous preconceived notions of who you were or expectations of who you needed to be?

When people travel or get a fresh start, this is what I believe people are seeking—getting away from the exhaustion of being inauthentic. Unfortunately, though, when they return, they morph back into their old ego patterns or conform to the most effective behaviour that they know will receive external validation in their new environment.

So much effort.

Exercise: Feeling your authenticity.

Close your eyes. In silence, repeat your name. And with the feeling of being fully allowed, spread yourself throughout the entire room. Allow yourself to take up space. Allow yourself to be free.

Feel inside; you have feelings, but they are not you. You have thoughts; you are not them. You have a body, but this isn't you either. You have a mind, but you are not your mind.

Look at your life from a bird's eye view; like a long timeline, observe all the information, the birthdays, the heart breaks, the achievements, every moment. Realise that you have been observing the entire time. *You are this observing presence.*

The mind has been so loud that it's been using you; you had no idea. Come to this moment; feel it; observe it from above. You were already waiting for you, right here.

Open your eyes now, and look at something in the room.

Close them down, and hold that image.

Does it get fuzzy? Can you see it at all?

See how hard it is to control the mind even when you want to?

Have you ever fallen asleep and thought about how your mind just won't stop? You have acknowledged right then that you have a mind. What about when you have fearful or anxious thoughts, the what ifs? How hard do you find it to stop them? These thoughts and anxieties highlight that you cannot stop your mind, *the mind,* not you.

It is something that can be tamed with practice, yes. But first, you must realise that it is something that can be used as an incredible creative machine. What you feed it and keep in it is what you will experience in the world around you. It is you that has this creative power. The mind is the paintbrush; your life is the painting. You are the one who gets to direct and observe it all.

Do you see the power in simple, authentic stillness yet?

Once you have had one of those 'holy fuck' moments when you realise that you are not your thoughts, you'll suddenly feel a freedom from the need to be validated.

The realm of egolessness is often referred to as the "death-less realm" by Buddha because the space between thoughts, the present moment, is always there. It never dies. In the realm, there is no thinking and, therefore, no ego. In this space between thoughts, you realise that you are already complete. Nothing is missing. There is nothing to add or take away.

This space means the death of the ego. But not really, because it will come back to life shortly.

Don't worry about the ego! Don't worry about it then, and don't worry about it now. It's probably still blabbering on in your head right now; am I right? It is probably arguing, con-fused, or wondering what your next meal is.

We waste so much energy upholding the sense of identity, the sense of me.

We waste so much time worrying about the past or the future.

Might I suggest that someone never willing to become still has never taken the first step towards truly living? But we can always give it a go. Try stilling the mind when you're out in pub-lic. Just sit back and be still. Observe the habitual need to com-ment. Notice your reactive and unconscious desire to have an opinion, to be seen, and to be heard.

Now, for the interesting part, **resist that reaction. Resist the need to be heard for a week.** See what happens.

Eventually, who you thought you were will seem like a shell. The old behaviour will seem childish and ugly in a sense.

Don't let the ego make a problem out of it, or a goal. As soon as there is a problem, your mind is in the past. As soon as there is a goal, your mind is in the future. You have suddenly opened the floodgates of thought again.

This experiment requires a deep commitment to remembering that the ego will compare, contrast, desire, judge, want, and fear. While those are all completely normal, they're only real when you give them your attention. Resist being pulled into focusing on them.

You don't have to give your thoughts your attention. Imagine your attention is a credit card with which you purchase your life experiences. Where you put your attention is what you're paying for and what you'll get in your life. If you're purchasing the lack-based thoughts of your ego with your attention, this is what you'll experience. But if you pay more attention to the present moment and accept what is, you go beyond your mind. Then you'll be purchasing more energy, more freedom, and a greater ability to be cool, calm, and collected.

In that space, there's no reputation to live up to, no person to compare yourself to, no baggage. Our reactions to people and events have nothing to do with the world around us and everything to do with the mental world in our mind, dictating what is right and wrong.

You are here to live, but you cannot fully live if you're trapped in the limitations of one-person beliefs, memories, experiences, and attachments. Live with them and through them. Use them, but don't be them.

There is no obligation anymore. Without your emotional patterning defining your likes and dislikes, wants and needs, you are free to use that energy that you used to be reactive, and you can live in peace.

This realisation that you don't have to do what your ego tells you makes authenticity so simple. Your ego doesn't control you. You can use your mind, your memories, and your knowledge, but they no longer run you.

Exercise: You Spot it; You Got it.

You can try this one anywhere.

Anytime when you feel triggered, which means you feel something emotionally shift within you as a negative charge, write down specifically what ticked you off.

Example: Sally ignores you at a lunch date with a bunch of friends. You are triggered because Sally was rude. (Remember that, in your mind, being ignored can mean something totally different to someone else, such as ignorant, selfish, narcissistic, etc.) Since our triggers are about what is not accepted unconditionally within ourselves, we care not for what it might mean to anyone else; we only care what it means to us at that moment. So, once you identify what it meant to you, it's time to examine yourself.

As Pema Chodron, ma girl says, "The most fundamental aggression to ourselves, the most fundamental harm we can do to ourselves, is to remain ignorant by not having the courage and the respect to look at ourselves honestly and gently."

Get out a pen and paper, and sit down with a cuppa and a notepad. Gently and honestly scan your past actions for every moment where you were (in this example) rude.

Write specific examples using full sentences. From the earliest times of your life until this very moment, jot them all down. By taking the time to do this, you are taking the time to free yourself from ignorance, pain, and blame. Keep writing until you can see that you have been rude in your life as well, to the same extent as Sally and, perhaps, differently yet still equally rude.

And then, close your eyes. Imagine rude as a part of yourself. Find that part of you in your body by breathing and doing a mental scan. Feel into the edges of your skin, and roll with whatever comes up. Once you find that part of you, I want you to imagine looking that part of you in the eyes and saying repeatedly, "I see you, and I love you. You are the yin to the yang of polite (or insert opposite of whatever trait that you are balancing), and you are a part of what makes me whole." This is called unconditional love, vulnerability, human authenticity, and acceptance of the reality of our flaws as a human. Repeat, I see you, and I love and accept you until you no longer feel shame, blame, or resistance.

Now go, and enjoy that instead of feeling triggered by people who are rude, you can experience compassion and go along our merry old life feeling unfuckwithable.

Needless to say, you can do this with anything that triggers you. Any blame or criticism, even with what may appear as the cruelest, unspeakable actions or traits that you recognise in another human. Recognising and owning them within yourself is a higher, conscious, empowered state of living. It gives you a choice, not justification for rude actions (rude in the example above), but a choice to act differently and recognize that it is only a trait in another. It is one part and not the whole. You can choose to not be near that person if you wish, but instead of judgment, you have awareness and love.

Pretty fucking cool, right?

Lesson
4

VULNERABILITY: Exercising Bravery Just to Be You Cultivates Confidence

"When you give yourself permission to communicate what matters to you in every situation you will have peace despite rejection or disapproval. Putting a voice to your soul helps you to let go of the negative energy of fear and regret."

—Shannon L. Alder

Vulnerability is where the alchemy of fear begins. To be vulnerable means to surrender into being seen with the collective, perfect imperfections, of what it is to be human. Vulnerability in its literal sense means being exposed to potential harm or pain.

In this case, it is rejection from others that represents the harm or pain. We show courage when we show up as our authentic selves and risk rejection or, more honestly, how we stomach rejection, for it is a very natural and normal part of life. These all require bravery.

From this moment on, know that every rejection you sustain, be it from friends, jobs, partners, or family, is simply life filtering out the bullshit that doesn't resonate with you. Rejection is like the qualification process in sales. Anyone who has worked in marketing knows that the better qualified the leads are, the more chance of happy customers and sales for the business; rejection = happy you that generates flow in life (business).

Think of it like this; you want quality, not quantity.

Rejection only hurts when we hold onto the belief that our worth is based on another's acceptance. You're probably figuring out by now how false that belief is. Courage and bravery never feel how they sound, by the way.

We have this warped image of knights in shining armour being courageous. In fact, to be brave is to be without armour, and courageous is what we can use to describe someone who does something that they are terrified to do.

Let me give this context:

People often say to me, "You're so courageous talking on stage. You make it look so easy." Well, this isn't courageous of me because speaking on camera or stage isn't something that scares me. Falling deeply in love with someone or taking a month off work terrifies me so doing those things would be courageous of me. Talking on stage? A piece of cake.

It's not courageous of me because it's easy for me. Courage is relative. What seems courageous to one person might be seemingly natural for another. Courage is very much the description that we can use after the fact, after we have faced our greatest fears.

Courage is the illustration of acting when we are shit scared. Like, showing up as ourselves fully, warts and all. Brave is what we must be before; courageous is what we become after. Neither feels like they sound.

Fake it till you make it, then?

Nah, just know that when you are peeing your pants, you're heading in the right direction.

An unfuckwithable life is one that often requires spare knickers!

Combine this knowledge with the sense of fearless authenticity, reached through a state of stillness, being totally and utterly present with life and who you are, and you have reached what I consider nirvana. To be connected and aware of your true essence as a soul *and* accepting of your wholeness as a human is enlightenment.

But why does vulnerability—that acceptance that we are whole—feel so painful?

Being vulnerable means admitting that the ego's sense of self could be questioned, challenged, or weakened. However, the ego is always looking for a way to strengthen its sense of self. Any challenge to the idea of who you are is a threat. Taking offense or feeling victimised is the ego's way of protecting itself.

Now, since vulnerability is a complete and utter knowing that we are the yin and the yang, which make up the whole, it is also a state of awareness. Accepting the whole *is authenticity.* Surrendering the mind while understanding the wholeness of it at the same time is epic. Here's why the ego's incessant self-preservation is a problem. If you can't move beyond the mind and surrender into vulnerability, you will never truly be able to have healthy relationships, be that a healthy relationship with yourself, another person, or the world around you. Being in a *healthy* relationship means not needing the relationship to make you happy, whole or full in any way. It doesn't take a psy-chologist to tell you that seeking happiness in someone else is going to end badly. You must be connected with yourself first. Fall head over heels in love with yourself.

Being full within yourself means realising that your weak-nesses, negatives, and perceived failures are the perfect other half of your wholeness. These negatives compliment your strengths, positives, and successes. Acknowledging this is to be vulnerable.

To be in a healthy relationship, it's equally important not to be reactive and defensive. If someone says, "You're selfish," being vulnerable allows you to observe yourself, check in on whether that's true or not, change your behaviour accordingly if you were acting selfishly, and get on with things. You can create healthy boundaries this way. *"Thanks for letting me know; sorry I was selfish."* That is authentic. How would the fearful ego-driven conversation go instead? Probably something like you throwing a tantrum, blaming something or someone else, and creating an enormous victim fight about it. I can hear it now, can't you? *"How dare you speak to me like that!"* You get the idea.

The thing with being vulnerable is you're essentially emotionally invincible and available at the same time. Here's an example. If someone were to call you a purple elephant with yellow spots, and you aren't, you wouldn't get offended. You would feel nothing because it's not relevant. There is no need to defend yourself or react. The ego would most likely carry on like an emotional dickhead, triggered by such a blow to its identity. However, a conscious person who's present and aware can just simply observe the reaction without feeding it.

As humans, we are made up of negative and positives aspects.

We have empowered personality traits, and we have disempowered ones.

We have dark emotional patterns, and we have light ones.

We fail in life, and we succeed.

We experience ups and downs, highs and lows.

Vulnerability is seeing that there is always both, but it requires bravery to admit that. Self-love begins with the decision to open up to the fact that, as a human, you will be imperfect in many ways. When you realise that being imperfect is both inevitable and normal, you don't give a fuck what anyone says! You can take feedback, process it for any potential growth that it offers, and let everything else go. It no longer will lead you to emotional reactions, no more scrambling into a pit of insecurities cunningly disguised as flashy watches, Netflix, or Ben & Jerry's.

This is the yin and yang of life, the two sides to the whole in this world of form.

It's important that you're prepared to become vulnerable first. Before moving on to the other codes, before you can fully digest love and accept yourself unconditionally, lead with your heart, and choose love, you must embrace the unfamiliar world of becoming vulnerable. Are you brave enough to surrender your ego? You are if you choose to be. (*See what I did there.*)

Without embracing vulnerability, you'll never be able to fully be authentic, because you will be stuck in your mind, stuck in judgment, stuck in fear of rejection, and stuck with the need for perfection. Your ego fears vulnerability because vulnerability is the realm where conscious awareness never dies and where thought and ego do not exist. Staying in your fear means that you will never truly be satisfied. You'll never be rich enough, pretty enough, successful enough, or happy enough, but never being truly satisfied means that you will never feel confident within yourself. You will always seek more. You will always feel insecure and unworthy of love. You will always need that external validation. You will always remain addicted to your internal self-assurance via the ego voice that is either *building up the self or critiquing it and bringing it down.*

On the flip side, vulnerability and realising your wholeness is the real path to unfuckwithable.

Lesson

5 | # HUMAN: Don't Forget Authenticity is Being Human Too

Remember that you are not always supposed to know everything.

Remember that you are not always supposed to have it all figured out. There is not one way, one truth, or one ultimate meaning for being here.

Remember that you are human, with beautiful flaws and scars and stories that are uniquely yours.

You are not here to move toward perfection or even mastery.

You are here to know what it means to be truly alive through the process of experimentation, adventure, experience, and extrapolation.

To catch a glimpse of the divine and lose it again, time and time again.

You are here to explore the things in your everyday, ordinary life that gets your heart racing, stomach fluttering, and body dancing with excitement—things that strike chords of truth deep within and awaken something almost inexplicable in the belly of your soul.

Throughout all the lessons and triumphs, successes and failures, never forget the limitations of being human.

Revel in the joy, frustration, ecstasy, and sorrow that accompany the experience of being alive.

To feel the pain in your heart or the heaviness on your shoulders is a reminder that you are here. You are alive. You have the choice.

Never forget to be sweet to yourself as you maneuver throughout your days because, darling, you are new here—

Not the eternal, deepest self, you, who has been here since the beginning of time,

But this you.

With this body and this mind.

With these past experiences, current struggles, and future projections.

Remember that your ultimate task isn't mastery, perfection, or success in the typically defined way.

Your ultimate task is

to experience,

to play,

to love,

through all the highs and lows, joys and sorrows, questions, doubts, self-criticism, and *a-ha* moments.

Remember that you, too, are simply human,

perfectly imperfect,

beautifully flawed,

complete in every single moment.

If you want to feel confident and unfuckwithable, you must realise this.

Avoiding looking at ourselves and asking ourselves who we are is not much different that avoiding the first jump into the cold water as spring leaves and summer arrives. It's scary; we don't know what to expect and most of all, we are afraid of what it will feel like.

But just like when your head breaches the surface, and you feel cleansed, when we hold the courage and dig a little deeper, under the anxiety and low self-esteem and ask what lurks beyond these emotions, we will discover the answers to our very freedom.

Why do we avoid feeling, introspection, and asking ourselves about ourselves? It is because we fear the answer. We fear not knowing or knowing and not liking what we find.

The answer, "I don't know," is the best place to begin.

To discover who you are authentically is to let go of all the different roles that you play to protect yourself. We put on a show to get the approval and love from others that we are not giving ourselves.

We must have the courage to put our armour of non-feeling aside, to see what is underneath, and to love every bit of it. Going deep is the secret.

We need to have the courage to be naked in our ugly under-wear and bear it all to the world. When you peel back the layers of emotions and the stories that bind us to the belief that we are not good enough, we see that underneath the armour we **are** imperfect.

We are hiding parts of ourselves through the fear of rejection, but it's this shame and guilt that give life to insecurity and fear. If you stop trying to hide the parts of yourself that are not perfect, you won't ever, ever, ever feel like you are not enough because you have accepted the reality that we all need to realise.

I am perfectly imperfect.

Lesson

6

SOUL:
Your Soul is Everlasting

We see references to the soul everywhere. It's all over the internet, and there are countless spiritual texts out there. But what does it mean—soul?

The best way to explain, perhaps, is to give an example of when we're best able to sense a soul and its existence. Think of a time when you have been around a newborn baby. You could feel a pure energy, couldn't you? There is no denying how special this little being is. Even the angriest old man cannot deny the pure essence of this tiny human.

While at our essence our souls are the same— awareness, something that cannot be described or understood by the mind, just felt, known and experienced—in children, we witness how unique we all are from birth. Babies are a single expression of this awareness. Anyone who has had younger siblings, multiple children, or interacts with newborns would have experienced this. It's as if each of us is born with a little somethin'-somethin' of our own before we even form a sense of me and my beliefs. When you can observe the mind and the ego's unconscious habits for self-strengthening, you can freely express this shining light without agenda.

The newborn has no name, no memories of who they were, are, or who they need to be. They have no expectations and no fears of failure. They are 100% who they authentically are.

Be like a child is a saying so clichéd when referring to consciousness, but that is exactly the state of a child, no thinking. Thoughts will form, and beliefs will form eventually, but that freshness of children is the essence of our soul.

Kids bring out the same sense of presence within us that art and flowers do. I believe that the reason we are attracted to beautiful things is to show us the way back to our soul. Of course, the ego turns beauty into something it wants to have—to own—and it has become a major source of validation and identity, especially in the Western world. But initially, in my view, all natural landscapes and forms of art and creativity, like dancing, singing, and painting are inner callings; they bring us home to who we are, to a state of presence from where we can truly express ourselves.

The child will soon develop a sense of self and begin to understand what behaviours give them validation and love and what behaviours take them away. Fear and self-sabotage begin at a young age and are based on how the child receives or does not receive love, feels or does not feel validated, what was or was not considered acceptable, what was relative and familiar, and what was right and wrong about life. I spend most of my coaching hours unwiring and releasing the pain that my clients suppressed as children and rules that we made up in our head about what it was to be good enough.

Exercise: Childhood Questions

Answer the following questions.

Who did you crave love and approval from the most as a child?

Who did you feel that you needed to be in their eyes to be enough?

The answers will give you an idea of where to begin bringing awareness to and where to observe. Through awareness, you will be able to let go of the most unconscious and fear driven aspects of your life. We usually mould ourselves according to the answer to question number two. Think about the answers to these questions again at these different ages: before 4, between 4-7, 7-14, 14-22 and 22-now. Replace "child" with the age bracket in question. Pay attention what comes up. Pay attention to the pain that you may or may not have allowed to write in your stories.

It's a fine line to walk—expression and awareness, but the more you do it, the more you will become aware of what is authentic and what is habitual ego-building. You can choose to express the behaviours that come from your core if you wish. As Drake said, "*Live without pretending. Love without depending. Listen without defending. Speak without offending.*"

Whenever you wonder, "who am I?" remember you are nothing, and you are everything. To be still and experience this is the entire reason that you were born. You come in as a soul, live as an imperfect human, and come home to your primary purpose through awareness.

Wayne Dyer, a legendary spiritual teacher, explains this so beautifully.

> *"So, there's a part of you that you can get a hold of, and there's a part of you that you can never get a hold of, and those are opposite things. Who are you? Which one are you? You are combinations of opposites. The Bhagavad Gita speaks about combining the opposites— about fusing, or melting if you will, into the oneness. I think we have a free will, and at the same moment, we don't. We have to live with that. It doesn't make sense intellectually, but that's because our intellect is always*

trying to come up with a logical, rational explanation for things. To do that, it puts labels on things. But once you label something, you've got twoness. You've got the label, and you've got what you're labelling. And there is only oneness in the Universe, even though we artificially believe in twoness."

—An interview with Wayne Dyer and Ray Hechandra

Lesson

7 | LONLINESS: Loneliness is a Normal Stepping Stone in an Authentic Life

I'm not going to lie. Sometimes, discovering who you are outside of who you *think* that you are can feel a little lonely.

> *"To find out what is truly individual in ourselves, profound reflection is needed, and suddenly, we realise how uncommonly difficult the discovery of individuality is."*
>
> **—C.G. Jung**

We experience a dissipating and gripping loneliness when we begin to strip away the ego. I have seen a lot of people go into a little loop of, "Who am I then?" I want to warn you that your ego will want to make a problem out of not knowing, but you do not need to do that.

Needing to know defeats the entire process.

It will be awkward to move away from who you think that you are. You'll resist against it and realise so much of what you were doing or who you were being was habitual. That identity will no longer fit like it used to.

Remember, habitual behaviour isn't bad. It can, however, lead us down a path of chasing more; the consequence of never observing yourself or figuring out who you are is an emptiness that is never filled.

At first, yes, there will be growing pains, but then you will be free. *[fist pump]*

The time taken up by this paralysing conundrum is different for each of us. For some, it is only moments. For others, it is years. And many people take their entire life. Think about Einstein. He was a complete loner, but he was incredibly authentic. His work continues to influence our lives to this day. He is a legend. And yet he was said to be depressed, desperate, and, frankly, quite weird.

"You have to be odd to be number one."

—Dr. Seuss

We feel this loneliness when we move towards authenticity because what was there before to protect us, the me-ness, is suddenly useless once you realise that it's a lie. It feels like a state of limbo. "I don't know who I am, so I am nothing." You must wait a few more moments to realise that when you let go of who you are, all of your options, your past, your beliefs, and attached emotions, you drop your lifetime of baggage.

So, is it worth it?

Just when the caterpillar thought the world was about to end, it became a butterfly.

It offends me. It offends us all. The falseness that we project to the world; the lies that we pretend are who we really are. It's an insult to all of us not to live our truth. We are all hiding from the same thing, being seen as us, without the act. But the only thing to fear is the insecurity of another, also afraid and projecting back. Give those people strength by ending the act. You must decide. No one can do it for you. Work towards breaking those old suppressive patterns. Step up. Stop being a kitty cat, or you will get to the end of your miserable, unfulfilled life and realise that you are miserable and unfulfilled and have been all along. Let people judge you. Let them criticise. Let them project their fears and insecurities and doubts. They will judge, reject, and criticise you regardless.

So, be you. I know it's scary as hell, but at least you will be living a life of meaning. It is the most unfuckwithable thing that you could ever do.

Lesson

8 | EVIL:
The Ego is Not Evil

"A man's mind may be likened to a garden, which may be intelligently cultivated or allowed to run wild, but whether cultivated or neglected, it must, and will, bring forth. If no useful seeds are put into it, then an abundance of useless weed-seeds will fall therein, and will continue to produce their kind."

—James Allen, *As a Man Thinketh*

Religion, a football team, a family, a nationality—all have a collective sense of who they are. Anything that creates a set of beliefs and opinions can be referred to as an ego.

So, wars are all ego. The need for more power, overruling, and seeking control over others are all ego.

For a long time, I thought this whole ego thing was a big selfish, self-absorbed alien in my mind that I was attempting to get rid of with some yoga, green-smoothie-drinking, and meditation. Finally, I realised that the negativity of the thoughts was not the ego; only the feedback of the *feeling* of lack that I was experiencing by believing every thought was real.

Let's look again at the two default ways that the ego makes itself important: puffing up and defending its sense of self by criticising, shrinking, or shaming another or by criticising, shrinking or shaming itself and making itself small. Both stem from comparison. Both lack vulnerability, which is acceptance of the negative.

The ego left unchecked is always attracting lack, due to its standard story being a variation of, "not enough." The mind and the ego are separate. Our mind is like the projector at the movies and our thoughts are the reel placed inside. Our 'reality' is the movie on the screen and our five senses are us experiencing the movie (life) which the ego filters fear over. So yep, we are the projector and the projection. When we don't consciously direct our thoughts or recognise the ego for what it is, our unconscious mind and the "no enough", is automatically the reel fed into the projector. To change our lives, we have to replace our reel (direct our thoughts and bring awareness to the ego). Yes, this means focusing on what we want and gratitude for what we have, even when the reality we see is the opposite. I know, cli-fucking-che', but also incredibly empowering. Emotions and subconscious beliefs also influence the 'reel', which I go into a little later on.

Exercise: **Three steps to overcoming the ego.**

This is the most effective process of stopping any spiral. Go get 'em, tiger!

Become aware of it.

- ○ Remember that right now is what we have, and we are seeing each moment with the thoughts of right now. If you want abundance, focus on what makes your life abundant now. If you want peace, focus on peace; if you want love and energy, focus on love and energy. Embody each, right down to your cells. You cannot just *think* these things; you must do what it takes to *feel* them. We can shift what we feel by shifting our focus. Feel it in an energetic way; imagine yourself at your smallest particle, which is an invisible vibrating vortex of energy that you can direct any way you choose, by using your thoughts.

Laugh at it.

- o Bring lightness, bring a sense of realistic consciousness of the cunningness and transparency, and make the ego something funny, a joke that you laugh at.

Have compassion for it.

- o Being that a lot of stories are connected to a deep pain from our childhood that we have not yet conquered or uncovered, we must bring awareness and hold space for the belief, allowing the deep fear and uncomfortable emotions to come up (anger, shame, sadness, pain). Then bring compassion to the story and the fear as if it's a little child and allow it to be felt and flow through you, and let it go.

Lesson

9 | ATTRACTION: Fear Based Beliefs Attract What We Don't Want

To be honest, I don't have the answers to manifestation. I have read all of Deepak Chopra's work and can quote *The Secret*; I can understand most of it, but the intricacies of it are complex—beyond the scope of this book. As a premise, we can assume that according to physics, there is always an opposite and equal reaction to each action, and likewise, that manifestation works backwards.

When we want something that is perceived as good, we are predisposing that something not good is bad. We create fear when we chase the good. Desiring the positive becomes a negative experience. Flip it now. Going back to vulnerability, if you are open to negativity, then negativity becomes null and void. If we are at peace and okay with the negative, the negative becomes positive.

Now, what if we apply this to the physical world? Rather than our emotional states of positive and negative experiences being dictated by our judgment, go negative experience and positive experience.

If you focus on what you do want constantly and repeatedly, your thoughts, actions, and energy will change. Your emotions shift; your biochemistry reacts to your mind; you appear different to people when you are focusing on something inspiring. You attract people who see and feel that. There is a lot of ancient research on manifestation, and I have a little picture to help wrap this all together.

Imagine this same law applied to the subconscious mind, which is the driving force of our thoughts and actions. "Sub" means "under", and "conscious" means "aware of." We can move *under* our *awareness.*

How do we get there?

You must train, discipline, and focus your conscious thoughts so that they seep into the subconscious.

One thought at a time enters the subconscious, which influences the potential action and result of your life. Add every thought up, every potential, every action, and you get the sum of these: your life.

If you don't prioritise stillness in your life and examine your thoughts, reactions, beliefs, and blame, how do you ever expect to be able to direct your life?

Now, what does the ego have to do with manifestation?

We know that the ego exists in duality, which is to say partial, separation, or half of a whole. It's always focusing on what's lacking.

Even believing the thought, "I don't know," will ensure you feel confused, and create and attract more things to confuse you.

Same goes for believing that you are not loveable or that you never finish anything that you start, that life is too hard, that you can't do it, that you are afraid of love, that you don't know how to make money, or that you are at the mercy of your genes. You get the idea. We know negativity all too well.

When running on autopilot, you're a magnet for things that prove the stories of fear that your ego tries to convince you is real. Sure, you can find evidence for it because you created it. Choose to change it by changing your focus, right now. The past only reflects the future if we live there. *You have no obligation to repeat the past.* You are not your past; you are not those stories; you are a ball of potential ready to be directed.

Your thoughts, feelings, emotions, and beliefs shift the energy of your world and in your world. If you don't choose consciously to interrupt the constant negative cycles in your mind, you will constantly attract lack.

To create the life that you want, you need to recognise your authentic self is not your mind and redirect your attention to connection within and to shift your beliefs, which adjust your emotions, which change your focus, which transform what you feel. Together, this is how you control what you get in life.

This is your power.

Lesson 10 | ARMOUR: Removing Your Emotional Protection Is Brave and Powerful

I used to misunderstand the importance of being compassionate or empathetic. Before learning about vulnerability, I wore thick emotional armour, which began to develop from when I was a child. I grew up between two households where, as a young girl trying to make sense of the world, I perceived the female role models as emotional, dysfunctional, and essentially something that I didn't want to be. So, instead of growing into my feminine essence, I powered through life like a gladiator, hunting for power, control, and freedom: the essence of masculinity. I avoided, judged, repressed, and resisted half of who I was; we are both masculine and feminine. I especially missed these characteristics within others, which lead to a great lack of empathy and compassion for others, and myself, and over compensation of narcissism, which is the opposite of empathy, and we all also have. Thus, I viewed emotional expression, showing weakness, making mistakes, failing, or getting less than first place or top marks as a waste of time. I also judged others who reflected any of these perceived weaknesses.

I was very fuckwithable; you might say. My entire life hung on the false perception of control, perfection, and power. Through years of work, meditation, yoga, mentors, meltdowns, breakthroughs, patience, persistence, travelling, love, heartbreak, reading, and, now, a (more) disciplined mind, I realise that a lack of vulnerability is the antithesis of strength.

Armour is a massive block when it comes to being unfuckwithable.

You are most fuckwithable when you have emotional armour on. We might appear strong, but we experience more shame, fear, and doubt. I would go as far to say that the more bullet proof the armour, the stronger the fear.

I have found that we all have emotional armour or experience a disconnection from our feelings at various levels; it's a part of the human experience as we explore and cling to safety and control. Spiritually speaking, disconnection is the thief of the greatest joys that we can embody.

Authenticity or to be unfuckwithable requires showing up humanly imperfect with emotions, feelings, flaws, faults, and fuck ups.

I did not realise how uncomfortable that I was with vulnerability until I reflect on the moments like the time that a client I was personal training cried when she got onto the scales. She was devastated about her weight. Being practical and wearing my armour, I saw her tears as wasting time and as preventing her from achieving her goal. My protected self though *she could be training with renewed motivation. Why did she need to cry about this?* This is a very masculine type of energy. No, not male, not man, just a masculine energy. "Fix the problem." "Do not engage in emotion." It shouts these messages without honouring the whole person.

I have always been overly practical until I learned the art of vulnerability and its key to a fulfilling and unfuckwithable life. I figure that a lot of the world, especially strong women, and, most of all, strong men, can relate. There is a documentary from the United States called *The Mask You Wear*, and it reveals the social conditioning about what it is to be a man. From this documentary, I was inspired to try a little de-armouring exercise, which focused on the concept of being unfuckwithable. Although I had spoken about vulnerability with many clients previously, I had never specifically gone for the jugular and drilled into their shame to test the theory specifically and to ask them how they felt before and after. So, I ran a little experiment with an excellent portrait photographer, Jason Malouin, to represent being unfuckwithable.

Jason shot the image used for the cover of this book. He's a fucking legend, making me look all unfuckwithable and open.

It's incredibly difficult and takes both talent and skill to capture someone's essence. Jason is a master at this. When we did our shoot, I described to him that I wanted people to feel complete acceptance and strength reflected to them when they saw the image of my face. He instructed me to look through the camera, not at it, but through it. Smile, but don't smile, express, but do not express. It felt so contradictory. Throughout the shoot, all I could think about were these two things: *I see you, and I love you.* I heard and said it repeatedly in my mind. These words reflect part of a process that I use for dissolving shame and integrating parts of ourselves that we have rejected for one on one clients.

I realised, again, how much effort it takes, due to conditioning, to show up authentically. How much I had not to try, how hard it was to be effortless. I was so used to doing me.

A bunch of people who trusted me to dive into their vulnerable spaces were invited for 30-minute intervention process to try this I see you, I love you concept. Each person only knew the length of time of the discussion and that we were going to take a before and after discussion photo of their face. They were familiar with my work, but this was a new concept to all of us.

The process was unique to each person.

At first, Jason took a few shots when he asked the people to show him variations of unfuckwithable. He asked them to show him unfuckwithable to an enemy, to a friend, to a stranger and other similar variations. He took shots of all of the variations.

Then, it was my turn. Using my tools from a variety of professional skills including a Diploma of Mindfulness Based Cognitive Behavioural Therapy, Neuro Linguistic Programming, and Deep State Repatterning Therapy, I dug into the uncomfortable place that I could see each person was resisting. I allowed them to guide me to a spot within themselves where they identified the part of themselves that they were rejecting. With a unique process, I essentially directed them to love and accept that part of them unconditionally. They were in a raw, vulnerable, and very grounded state by the end. When we finished, I asked them to open their eyes, and Jason took the shot.

Aesthetically speaking, the first shots are what you might see in a fashion magazine. The second, perhaps in moments of miracles. It was like watching your child win a gold medal, holding a newborn, or having someone you love tell you they love you back. You may have felt what I am referring to, moments where your heart is filled with so much love that it wants to burst open. You were raw, revealing, and deeply connected. I reviewed the before and after photos with each client. When I asked, "Which did you feel most vulnerable in?" and, "Which do you feel truly confident and unfuckwithable in?" every single person, without hesitation or even a speck of doubt, pointed to the after shot. It made me so fucking happy.

It was an absolute reflection of the very message that I want to get across in what I teach. Unfuckwithable is in a state of utter vulnerability, unconditional love, and self-connection even though it is uncomfortable, uncertain, and even scary at first. When we become whole through surrender, we are unfuckwithable.

Our greatest strengths, power, and purpose come from removing our armour and dropping the facade.

LOVE AND ACCEPT YOURSELF UNCONDITIONALLY

INTRO: Unconditional Love Makes for an Unfuckwithable Life

Unconditional means without conditions.

Meaning: love and accept no-matter-fucking-what.

Whenever you have a but after I love myself, this implies conditions. It is simple as a concept, but for our minds, conditioning is all it knows. Being loveable, enough, worthy, and acceptable, no matter what, in spite of, or even more powerfully, because of, our authentic, perfectly imperfect nature is foreign to the ego because nothing is ever seen how it is in its eyes. Instead, the ego sees things for how they should be or need to be.

The question is not, "how do I love myself unconditionally?" but an act of remembering that the only conditions around love are those of the ego. Therefore, they are untrue.

Here are some questions to help you see where conditional love is so transparent. If you answer no to any of these, or anything similar of the sort, you have conditions around love. These reservations mean that shame lurks in your being and that subtle longing to run from that discomfort is whispering at you, *"wine will fix it," "work harder," "you'll feel better when you have a tight butt and lean figure."*

Would I love myself if I never represent the body of the front cover of magazines?
Would I love myself if I had no money?
Would I love myself if I were dumped by my partner?
Would I love myself if I didn't have all the answers?
Would I love myself knowing that I have hurt people's feelings in the past?
Would I love myself if I got fired?

There is no right or wrong in actions or within ourselves. There is only the way that the mind perceives a situation. The end is that we can all go home now. Not really, but honestly, that understanding alone, if you can appreciate and apply it, will give you a sense of freedom from doubt and insecurities that you probably only thought was possible after 10 espresso martinis.

One of the biggest resistances that I come across in people when it comes to unconditionally loving themselves is that they will lose their drive in life around a goal. For example, when I was working with a client who had been diagnosed with anorexia, she was terrified to love her body because she feared that if she did, she would eat too much food and get fat. Our egos resist unconditional love because it would mean that we would finally be enough. We could stop doing, changing, and, most of all, hiding the parts of ourselves that aren't perfect. When we are identified with the ego voice of our thoughts, we are so used to being driven by pain and fear that we are terrified that if we don't hate, reject, or criticise a part of ourselves, we will relax into life enough and be content. Imagine that.

When we swap fear and resistance for love and acceptance, we end up with inspiration. And instead of being motivated to be better or because you don't feel enough, you are being inspired by love and gratitude for yourself and life, and you access a magnificent flow. You work smarter, and the body, the money, and the success become bonus side effects of this flow.

Knowing yourself and knowing what you are inspired by means that you can live from a place of pull towards something rather than a place of pushing against yourself and against life to get somewhere else. The first is moving towards life; the other is shrinking away.

Unconditional love makes the term love seem insufficient, but in our world of conditions, I felt it necessary to bring to our attention to our relationships, be that with our friends, family, intimate partners or ourselves; our society has slapped conditions all over love.

Whether conscious or unconscious, many have come to accept conditioned love as normal. We don't have to accept it. Love with conditions is ego love.

To reintroduce real love back into your life, I have added the word unconditional next to it.

We are all seeing and mirroring ourselves to one another. What we are triggered by is either parts that are consciously in our mind or parts that we believe we do not have. That stands true for both negative and positive lacks. For example, you hear a story about someone cheating on their partner. You're triggered, and you judge them. That trigger is a sign that that person is reflecting to you a part of yourself that you've not owned and accepted unconditionally as part of your human traits. You judge it and resist it within you, so, therefore, you judge it in another.

On the flip side, you hear a story of someone else's incredible success. You feel anxious, jealous, and depressed by this. That triggering is a sign that you have not owned your ability and potential to create such success and reflect as much greatness into the world.

Either way, our triggers are our guideposts to love and accept ourselves fully.

Judgment reflects someone's deep insecurities. Insecurities are a perceived lack, not a real lack. Nothing is everrrrr lacking. *Nothing.*

I had this crazy dream once. It was an open space kind of dream where I don't remember the surroundings, just this giant white, 4D, paper cut out. It didn't have a gender or a face; it was just a plain, white cut out like the ones we made in year four at school when we folded a piece of paper multiple times and cut it out and then unraveled with a bunch of people holding hands. In my dream was a single, giant one of those. So, I was looking at it, and I knew that it was me in a way. Then, I saw it split into billions upon billions of tiny versions of itself, or myself.

This is the best explanation for each of us all being made up of the same parts. All traits and behaviors are part of each human. The choosing of love comes from being able to consciously remember to *choose love* always.

Give yourself the kind of love that people write books about.

For many of us, we ignore the subtle cries for what our hearts most want because of the wounds that we have yet to heal.

We continue to search for love in all the wrong places hoping that one day what we want will magically manifest itself, yet, this rarely occurs.

You must believe that you are worthy without having to know why. And you must believe that it is possible, without having to know how.

The love and emotional nourishment that we try to find through validation is the love that every human being deserves to receive. Therefore, it is essential that you learn to give this love to yourself.

The resistance to loving ourselves is not caused by an external influence, be it fitness models, millionaire entrepreneurs, or a happy couple who we are comparing our lives too. It's not even something that we lack within. It's a lack of connection.

Love is an untamed force. When we try to seek it outside of us, it destroys us. When we try to imprison it, it enslaves us.

Without unconditional self-love, you will search endlessly for love from somewhere outside, and when you are disappointed or rejected, validation will become the obvious and destructive substitute.

Eventually, you substitute all terms of true fulfilment with booze, pizza, and empty sex.

You can most certainly find external support systems for inner acceptance. Friends and mentors can be good examples of an external support system; however, they must be chosen wisely. We become the people who we surround ourselves with.

Find friends who call you out on your shit, not ones who whine with you. Choose friends who make you feel more alive not because they validate you but because they challenge you, by reflecting your greatness. What your ego sees as their success that you don't have is a reflection of your untapped potential. The anxiety around it is an energy catalyst waiting to be used.

You have two choices; you can listen to your mind about how you'll never be as incredible or pull your shit together, come back to authenticity and stillness, and take action to unleash your greatness. Choose friends who don't pretend that life is perfect, but make it infinitely more interesting through making mistakes and fucking up and getting through the tough times together, admirably.

Lastly, the people who you wouldn't choose to hang out with unless you wanted to spiral into negativity, will probably have very little understanding about themselves and the mind—the same place we all begin—so they will probably project their insecurities onto you as a coping mechanism. It's not justified, no, but we can choose to exercise compassion and understanding. They're doing the best they can with what they have, and we can choose not to take this personally.

If you sense someone is judging you, smile, and give them a compliment.

It's probably been an incredibly long time since someone showed them that kind of unconditional love.

You'll change their life.

Most of all,

You'll change yours.

Love and acceptance have very little to do with self-love and a lot to do with the understanding that there is nothing to not love, only a perspective to change.

You have probably heard, "Love your flaws," or, "Let go of past failures."

Technically, if we look at life with a truer perspective, that is to expand our perceptions beyond the automatic duality of the mind, we will see that our perceived flaws and failures are pieces of the pie that make us whole. Mm, pie.

Sorry, distracted.

What this means for us is that instead of thinking in terms of, "I must accept my imperfections, failures, and mistakes," we need to begin experiencing life with an open mind.

Love refers to a wholesome view.

And as Winnie-the-Pooh says in response to Piglet's question of, "How to spell love?" "You don't spell it, you feel it."

Acceptance refers to surrendering. If we can observe the world the way in which it is, not the way in which we are and the way that our mind sees, projects, analyses, filters, subjectively judges everything, we become open to life, open to success, open to an overflow of self-confidence, and open to unfuckwithableness.

When we practice taking off our filters of self-identity and seeing the world in a responsible and empowered way, we will see that even the darkest and deepest of wounds that we endure are balanced by understanding that the deeper the wound means, the more light that can get in.

I first thought of the name of this code as *Love and Accept Yourself Unapologetically* because it sounded kick ass at the end. We can get so deep in insecurities that a little, cheeky attitude of a Beyoncé finger wag will do us a world of good. You know, bringing things back into balance.

Speaking of balance, that's why I changed the title.

Love and acceptance can become like a credit card without a limit, a tool that you get to purchase whatever you want in life when you learn how to use it. There are four major elements that we must use with conscious attention to make us unfuckwithable: beliefs, emotions, feelings and thoughts. I spoke about these at the end of the last code, so let's expand on them now. When all four are congruent, life has an organic, rhythmic flow.

Sabotage is our conscious losing to the subconscious. It is when thoughts get overthrown by our beliefs.

Why? Beliefs can shift our state and trigger emotions, and they're enormous energetic vibrations.

You can feel the power of emotions when you are in a situation that makes you nervous, afraid, and even ecstatic.

They affect how we act, think, perceive, and experience the world.

Physically, emotions and thoughts can change the chemistry of our body and can wire our brains to link meaning to the world around us.

To love and accept yourself is like being the alchemist of your life.

You must learn to take a negative perspective, the negative parts of yourself, and negative situations, event, emotions, and experiences and find the positive partners to bring peace in your mind, body, and spirit. You must take what you have been given and make gold.

Like Nicola Tesla says, "If you want to find the secrets of the universe, think in terms of energy, frequency, and vibration."

If we are particular about where we direct our energy, we can stand in our power and shift our life.

Trying to figure out the universe with a mind is like asking a computer to check in with its intuition. It won't compute. So then, the animal part of us registers, "I don't understand this; it must not be safe." And our emotions compute, "Danger, danger," which then our brains often interpret as "Bullshit."

To be able to fully appreciate and utilise this code, you'll need to get out of your noggin. Don't worry too much if the whole feeling thing is a new concept; there is another chapter for that later. For now, just know that if you feel resistance, it's just because it's new.

Love and acceptance aren't just about loving yourself like some feminist revolution movement gone wrong. Love and acceptance exist on a much bigger scale, a universal acceptance of life. Love and acceptance require embracing the single most important truth.

Everything that is a part of the human experience, our very selves, emotions, events, and beliefs all comprise two opposing halves. Like two atoms bonding together to make a molecule, they need one to be negatively charged and one to be positively charged to attract and create. It's the same with our lives. As soon as there is enough energy to break apart the bond, it shifts form.

We know a couple of things to be certain in this world. All things are held together in our immediate universe that we walk and talk and think in by equal opposites. It's basic physics. Energetically, all things require equal positive and negative values to exist. What does this have to do with love?

Well, love in terms of life and being unfuckwithable has nothing to do with romance and everything to do with taking responsibility for your sense of inner peace and joy, by seeing what is there.

Simply put, emotional pain, and physical pain as the domino effect, are reflections of our mental perspective that only sees the partial picture.

In this life, we will be in a constant place of opportunity to either move back into the past and repeat it or move into the present and create it.

Let's get one thing straight.

Love and acceptance aren't an excess of empathy or compassion. No, they are simply the gatekeepers that open the doors to inner freedom and healing. Love and acceptance are not giving up, being walked over, being weak, or blindly being a doormat.

Love and acceptance require a deep amount of inner discipline and strength to let go of a perspective that sees a person, an event, or an item and challenge an emotion.

Love and acceptance are bold; they're powerful, and it takes a lot of courage. Like water, it can cut through even the toughest of elements, through persistence and dedication.

Love and acceptance are about letting go of painful stories that have held together part of an identity that's been living in pain, stimulated from said stories.

Love and acceptance are about integration, and they're about understanding the reality of our lives, which are made up exclusively of equal opposites. Emotional pain rises when our perspective is lopsided. It's missing a piece of the pie, so to speak.

It requires courage because the strongest parts of the human identity are often made up of the negative stories playing on repeat in our subconscious mind. The stories are so intertwined with who we think we are; we tend to defend the pain by blaming others, never wanting to let go of that part of us. Pain is like super glue. But love, like water cutting through stone, can loosen the deepest of sufferings with persistence and patience.

There are three ingredients to letting go of any pain:

- Knowledge
- Compassion
- Empathy

And the cooking element is the *application*.

It takes courage because there seems to be the belief within us that anger, blame, and shame towards another lessens the painful blow. It isn't true. Holding onto blame, shame, and anger towards someone who's action has left you feeling hurt or uncomfortable, is like holding hot coals and excepting that other person to get burnt. It only affects you.

We have the leverage ourselves. Sometimes, a good talking to our ego is necessary, like "Look, buddy, I know that what happened was rough, but if we keep this shit within us, it'll just stay on repeat. Given, it will gain our attention and significance; however, we're only going to keep on getting more miserable and decay away on the inside if we don't choose to let it go." We think that staying hurt will hurt them; we believe at some level that our pain is payback, but it won't, and it's not. It just destroys our life.

Pain is an addictive, internal comfort for many of us without us even realising it. A lot of what goes on, around 97%, per Dr. Bruce Lipton is subconscious.

Pain is so very powerful. It is one of the greatest catalysts for transformation and spiritual awakening for humans.

If we choose to let it be, of course.

Because of the equal opposites in this universe, the depth of pain that we experience is a reflection of the level of pure joy that we can reach within ourselves once we move through it.

Often, you don't know the value of air until you have gone without it.

When you go through an experience that burns like the fires of hell, the relief of pain is like taking a pair of heels off that have been causing blisters for the past 12 hours. It's fucking brilliant.

Love and acceptance are appreciating that at some level, we chose to walk through the fires of hell so that we can learn what it's like to feel fully alive.

> *"Because one believes in oneself, one doesn't try to convince others. Because one is content with oneself, one doesn't need others' approval. Because one accepts oneself, the whole world accepts him or her."*
>
> **—Lao Tzu**

Lesson

11 | TRUTH: To Love and Accept Yourself is To See The Truth

Love. Accept. No conditions.

To accept is to be conscious, to surrender, to be present, and to be enlightened.

To do this without an apology is your inner purpose, and your inner purpose is not something that you should ever apologise about. (More on that later.)

To love and accept are to realise that the good and the ugly parts combine to make a whole. You see the left foot and right foot. Unless you have two left feet, in that case, your life would suck; there's just no hope for you, sorry.

It's to see the pea and the pod, the peg and the hole. There is no moment, no person, no event, no situation that ever, ever, ever, ever, ever has more or less of one (beautiful) or the other (ugly). Usually, we seek wholeness from the outside in by trying to cover up the ugly parts of ourselves or our lives. This will only bring more ugliness. What we run from runs to us.

Love and acceptance are the most underestimated techniques in existence for releasing shame, anger, guilt, and resentment and building inner strength, inspiration, and confidence.

The world around you is all the same shit, just a different form, a different expression of the soul. In this way, to love and accept yourself is to love and accept others as well.

It is plain and simple, written in every instance of this life. There is no wrong without a right, no good without a bad, no up without a down, and no villain without a hero. They all exist in each one of us and every experience.

Both sides are there every moment. You just have to look at it a little differently to see it.

Our need to be right without wrong, successful without failing, beautiful without ugliness, happy without sadness, high without the low is the foundation of our worry and insecurity. And the rejection of **half of life**, of ourselves and others, cultivates in our life the parts that we are trying to run away from.

So, quit *striving* to be; quit standing for and seeking the positive without the negative because they're the opposites that always exist. It's your addiction to the fantasy—your constant needing and striving for this impossibility—that causes emotional turmoil.

Acceptance is surrender. Surrender is not a weakness like most of us think. Surrender is strength. It takes so much courage to love and accept ourselves at first because the mind will want to fight for is the distinction, to have an opinion, to be right by being right (the victor) or be different by being wrong or having wrongness (the victim). Surrender takes courage because it's purely living your authentic purpose and having an opinion but not having an agenda about it needing to be heard or known.

You cannot escape half of life, half of yourself, or half of another person. Your pain, my pain, the world's pain can dissolve, the moment that you surrender; the second that you choose to love what's there is the second that you realise that to be authentic is to be whole and to be whole is to see both sides of the coin. You can be powerful through love, acceptance, and inspiration instead of fear and the need for more significance, or the need for more anything.

It's not so easy to see this, though, when we are so conditioned and so deluded by our mind. But we have a choice.

We can choose to see the wholeness of everything.

It requires practice, patience with yourself, and patience with others. It requires knowing that no one is perfect. You are not yet perfect in this practice, and that is, well, perfect. It requires you to trust that you and everyone else are always doing the best they can with what they have.

When you can do this with yourself, with your past, your present and potential future, you can experience enlightenment. You will be so confident, vibrant, attractive, happy, relaxed, energised, and inspired. There is no fucking magic pill for happiness, no plastic surgery or super yacht that can substitute for the fulfilment that love and acceptance will bring you, or even just the practice of love and acceptance.

You will see the magnificence that you are made of. You will see yourself in the people who you previously resented or were irritated by. You'll realise that we are the same, just with different experiences, walks of life, and ways of revealing our soul. We are all here figuring out life. You can find gratitude in your past when you used to feel the victim. You can surrender, let go, and really live.

You can be free.

Lesson

12 | YOU: Love Starts With You

A wise person once told me that my only focus should be to fall head over heels in love with myself.

And he was right. I'm not sure if I will ever truly master complete unconditional love for myself, but it is something that I remind myself of regularly.

That's life. Practice is all that we must do to do it right.

Effortlessly, we must bring our intentions to what matters.

Right now.

Acceptance.

Wholeness

Love.

What does this look like?

You are the only person in this entire universe who can tear yourself down. I am the only one who can tear myself down. I refuse to let either of us think that anyone else can pull us down in this world, ever. The moment that we think there is something outside of us responsible for how we feel is the exact moment that we toss aside our happiness and throw our conscious magnificence in the dirt only to squish it like a used cigarette butt.

Why do we do this?

Well, who told us back when we were at school that we could change our life or that we were responsible for changing how we feel?

No one. No one told us, but someone told me, and now I'm telling you.

So, let's stand the fuck up, raise our heads from shame and worthlessness, and no longer allow our minds to tear us down.

What is lost when we love ourselves?

We lose the shit that we didn't know we were holding onto. We let go of the pain, the doubt, the addictions, the struggles, the abandonment issues, the fear of not enough. Every moment you choose the act of loving yourself releases the limitations that you used to define yourself.

Begin to see that the moment you entered this universe was the exact moment when you became perfect enough, worthy of all things great and wonderful. Learn to let go of the relationships with the world around you that are not based in authentic love.

Letting go doesn't come easy. In fact, this usually sets off some triggers in the world around you. This can potentially cause mayhem!

I lost friends who I thought were lifelong partnerships because I decided that it was more important to love me than go along with their stories.

I ended client contracts because I refused to shrink away from love and refused to fuel their fear.

I missed out on a massive investor because I wanted to present all of me to the world, and it was too risky for them when my entire self was seen.

Sorry, you cannot have me in parts. I am a full package.

It is an upside-down concept, letting go of who we needed to be and showing up as who we are with conviction, despite losing people along the way. But I gained so much sense of myself over the years of loving me. I gained so many quality, authentic clients, friends, relationships, and business partners.

It's time for you to step up to the diamond and get served your pitch, a pitch that asks you to stop shying away and letting your fears smother your innate knowingness that you are loveable, great, and have something to contribute to this world. I want to invite you to show up more than you ever thought was possible every single day of your life.

Loving ourselves doesn't always come easy, and that's not just a mental reference. It's hard to let go of what could be, might be, or should be, but we must let go to open up the space to invite what is meant to be. Sometimes, we need a mirror to see the perfection in the parts of ourselves that we have been rejecting.

Loving yourself isn't for the faint-hearted. The most successful business owners, filthy rich entrepreneurs, inspired speakers, and rock star mums realise that loving themselves is a must to access true potential and come from an authentic place of fulfilment and inspiration.

Lesson 13 | RUN: What We Run From Runs to Us

"Nothing ever goes away until it has taught us what we need to know... nothing ever really attacks us except our own confusion. Perhaps, there is no solid obstacle except our own need to protect ourselves from being touched. Maybe the only enemy is that we don't like the way reality is now and therefore wish it would go away fast. But what we find as practitioners is that nothing ever goes away until it has taught us what we need to know. If we run a hundred miles an hour to the other end of the continent to get away from the obstacle, we find the very same problem waiting for us when we arrive. It just keeps returning with new names, forms, manifestations, until we learn whatever it has to teach us about where we are separating ourselves from reality, how we are pulling back instead of opening up, closing down instead of allowing ourselves to experience fully whatever we encounter, without hesitating or retreating into ourselves."

—**Pema Chödrön,** *When Things Fall Apart: Heart Advice for Difficult Times*

Life always has a way of helping you find what you need.

It doesn't always feel or look pleasant.

It certainly hurts at times, but only if we ignore our intuition.

The less we pay attention to ourselves and the less we listen to our authentic self, the harder life will feel.

Mental perspective and actions are the two actions that we choose that have the ability for life to ripple back to teach us every thought that you believe or let stay in your mind. Every action that you take has a ripple effect on your body and your life, like a stone dropped in a pond; once it reaches the edges, it will ripple back to you.

Simply put, this is the law of creation that many spiritual teachers and some incredible scientists and doctors have written and spoken about for centuries.

Whether you put it down to creative essence or practical cause and effect, life is always teaching you; you are always teaching you. Therefore, we know that we create all of our experiences.

Instead of pouring your heart into the world around you and looking for validation, today,

Look at your reflection.
Look at your body.
Look at your life.
Look at your achievements.
Look at your failures.

And pour your entire heart into that, every single broken and imperfect piece.

Begin there, because those are the hardest parts to love, but they are also the parts where we hold the stories that keep us small, angry, sad, and lonely.

We fear that our brokenness makes us unworthy. In fact, we are never broken. To be perfectly honest, the shit that makes you feel broken is the shit that makes you whole.

The parts of you that you feel aren't good enough balance the parts that you flaunt, trying to make the world see you that way and that way alone. But it's this false story of perfection that keeps you a slave to insecurities.

If only you realised that humans are *meant* to be great and weak all at once, that this is what makes us one then you'd stop pretending to be perfect. You'll finally feel the weight of the world drop off your shoulders.

So, this is your permission to let it go of the story that you aren't enough.

We are all both parts of the doughnut. Mm, doughnut.

The ring *and* the hole. If you accept that the hole makes you who you are (as a doughnut, obviously) and it's *meant* to be that way, you will stop trying to shove cream in the middle and call yourself a custard tart.

Balance.

It's everything. It's all of us.

If you reject one or the other, you are lying to yourself, and that includes those times when you're too humble. These lies will cause excess emotional turmoil and fear. So, just roll with your shadow sides. Be okay with not being okay all of the time. Own those parts; love them; accept them, and they won't hurt you.

Fall in love with you. Fall in love with all of you. Pour your heart into every piece of you. You deserve it.

You deserve to be happy. I give you permission.

Lesson

14

MISERY: The Root of All Misery is Non-Acceptance

Life wants us to succeed, but we keep screwing ourselves over with our need to be right or our need to be wrong. Don't forget that to have problems also means to be important.

Every transformation that I have ever seen comes from a shift in perspective. This shift in perspective is why gratitude can be a transformative healing tool (Demartini).

Your emotions are a physical expression of what you believe.

If you feel happiness or something on the positive bandwidth of emotions, it's because you see, or perceive, more things that are right, or more things that are good, or more things that are wonderful, or more things that benefit. If you feel sadness, it's because the opposite is true.

Growth is not painful. *Resisting* growth is painful. The pain is part of the process, but it's the resistance that hurts. Pain is fear activating within our emotional body as we resist change and fear of the unknown. Letting go is not painful. Not letting go is what burns you. Holding onto the lies that bind your ego and control your emotions burns you.

Circumstances hurt when you resist them, when you don't want them, when you try to push away what you don't want, or when you run and hide and blame. *That's* when it hurts.

But if something is an arse in your life, an arsehole of a boss, a $400 phone bill, an unexpected breakup, a lying best friend, it only hurts if you try not to want it. If you just simply know it's there, accept it for what it is, and either do what you can to change or simply move on, it won't hurt anymore. When we focus on just the loss and not the gain, we will experience pain. When we see the loss and the gain, we are grateful— not elated, but grateful, peaceful, and calm. The difference between acceptance and non-acceptance is the difference between experiencing the hurt, pain, and sadness as it moves through you, with a deep sense of understanding that the desire to run and control is the perception that there is one better outcome than another, a better emotion than another. Through acceptance, you can experience the emotional pain and be present during a traumatic event—big or small—but not be controlled by it.

You are always creating and attracting exactly what you need to evolve. Letting go is so much harder than holding on, but holding on is far more painful.

When we hold fear within us, it sucks the life force from us. We attract more things to be fearful of. It drains our energy. We attract people on this same blocked path and life gets pretty fucking dull, but mostly, people accept it as just life.

Fuck that. Life is more than something to put up with. I want you to have the freedom that's at your fingertips, something that can transform your entire life.

Whatever we reject, we attract. Whether we are rejecting something within ourselves or something within someone else, or whether we still hold pain, anger, and blame towards an event that happened in our past, we will attract more of it unless we let it go.

It may appear that rejecting and letting go are the same, but they're in fact completely different. Letting go is not giving into the need to control, change, figure it out, compare, solve, overthink, worry about, fear, judge, and all the other pleasantries of the ego nature. Letting go is not doing rather than doing these processes. It is no longer giving attention to the thoughts. Even if it's not understood, to let go is to release it with acceptance.

To reject is to use one or multiple of the 7Fs to avoid surrender and acceptance. Note that this is almost always automatic, so you've got to be a detective to spot when you are rejecting.

We are our own teachers, subconsciously attracting the things that we have rejected to teach ourselves that we need to love and accept what has happened or what we are seeing.

When we love and accept the parts of ourselves that we have believed or currently believe are wrong, when we accept them as normal, human, and balanced, then we are immediately allowing them just to be. That's when they'll no longer be all-consuming for us. They'll arise and exist, but they won't control us.

When I realised that the parts of myself that I reject, and are triggered or pissed off or threatened, are the cause of my insecurities and anger, I could choose whether I continued to reject, blame, and judge, or own those parts and be free.

I always wanted to hold on and blame. My ego would be furious at the mere suggestion that the insecurities or hurts that I felt were coming from within me. Taking responsibility and letting go is courageous. It takes so much more humility, but it's the only thing that will ever truly let you enjoy life.

When you look inside yourself and accept responsibility, it's like taking away that extra weight that previously made you feel irritated, depressed, stressed, and angry. You will have the energy to go in the direction of your dreams, and you'll stop feeling like the entire world has it out for you.

Wouldn't that be nice?

Like I said, it's easier to hold on than let go, at least for a while. I am still challenged to practice this daily. But if you try, you'll see that you're exactly where you need to be, and you have all the answers.

Trust yourself.

Love and accept yourself.

Let it go.

Lesson 15 | HARMONY: Unconditional Love Brings Harmony

When we reject any part of yourself, an event, or someone else it will continue to show up in life repeatedly until we learn to love and accept it. We call it fate.

As painful as it is, imagine realising that we are responsible for everything that has happened to us. That everything has not happened for a reason but has a specific purpose to teach us what we need to love, what we have filtered, judged, and rejected, and what we need to accept.

The core root of depression is wanting something other than what is. Directly observed, it's resistance, the ego's subtle way of building on itself. If the ego accepted what is, it would have no purpose; it would surrender, and it would meet its death.

The victim mentality of feeling as though something has happened to me is the ego resisting what is. It has judged what is as negative or positive. From a higher state of observation, we can see that the positive and the negative make up two sides of the same coin.

Of course, nothing is right or wrong; rather, it is more pleasurable or more painful. This includes every perceived traumatic event or experience and happy situation that has ever occurred. Everything in this world is whole; it's only the ego perception, blurred through the bias of positive or negative, that makes it less than the whole.

Suffering is a sure thing if our mind is running us. When I say mind here, I am referring to the combination of thought and emotion as an interconnected thing. Thoughts trigger emotions. Emotional pain is merely the perception that something is missing. If it's perceived that an outcome is more positive than negative, we experience a positive emotion. We want more of it and run towards it. And if the ego perceives there is more negative than positive in an outcome, we experience a negative emotion. We crave less and run away. Then starts the cycle of attracting what we don't want that I spoke of earlier.

To work through past trauma, whether the loss of a loved one, a car accident, bankruptcy, something from childhood, abuse, divorce, or bullying, you must revisit it. You revisit it to bring the event into equilibrium—to find the balance. This is often referred to as gratitude. If it was a negative experience, you might have resisted feeling it, and therefore, it becomes stuck in your energy. If you can search into the situation and discover what's already there, the positive sides of which you can only currently see negative, the emotion experience won't be a positive one because you see the exact balance of the whole. You won't want more of it, and you won't want less. You are just grateful and accepting of the event. Knowing this truth allows us to trust and surrender to life; when things appear shit, we can trust that there is an equal benefit; we just haven't found it.

If only we could realise that emotions are a completely normal part of life. More importantly, they come with great messages, like red flags, begging for our attention, telling us to look here, or that they need to be heard.

Demartini plainly describes disease in a similar way. He says that thoughts, which influence our emotions and vice versa, trigger biological processes that stimulate the production of disease. I have seen this repeatedly in my clients, the repetition of old patterns, of old pain, of the blame on others, of rejection within themselves and life. These patterns will show up on their doorstep repeatedly until the trait or occurrence is loved and accepted. I've also seen that the patterns will show up in different ways and with increasing intensity as time goes on.

This is quite possibly the hardest concept for someone to grasp because the ego's major existence depends on blame and being the victim. Nevertheless, let go. Become grateful. See the *necessity* of both sides, good and bad, of every event, situation, person, and even yourself. Doing so means to surrender completely and to accept. Gratitude, of course, drum roll... makes what we have enough. This means truly seeing the wholeness of what is.

The ego's destruction is equality and acceptance.

It's why letting go can be so hard.

Because that would make us, well, equal.

You wouldn't be wrong or right.

You would just accept and love.

How boring, the mind would say. How boring, I used to say!

"It's more fun and exciting to fight for what you believe in."

This agenda is the silent killer. It's draining. It's exhausting. It feels powerful at first, but it comes at the price of an empty kind of satisfaction. For the ego, surrendering is about as nice as rubbing salt into a wound.

You could remove so much pain, misery, depression, and stress from your life if you looked at life and lived it with an attitude of love and acceptance. Your ego would fucking hate a simple state of surrender.

Lesson
16 | MULTIFACECTED: Your Fears Show Up in Different Forms Until You Stop Feeding Them

Through my early teenage years, I had this fear that if I didn't grow boobs, I would never get a boyfriend. I stuffed tissues in my bra and wished every day for boobs.

And then later when I had boobs, I had a fear that if I wasn't skinny and muscly instead, men would find me unattractive. I had an appalling relationship with food fuelled into the escaped obsession with running, in its literal sense, outdoors, on treadmills, and up and down stairs. I ached in my joints. I overtrained. I worsened my adrenal fatigue, and everything hurt. Now that I had boobs, I had found something else to worry about.

Later, I had a fear that if I quit my degree-level job and worked for myself, people would devalue me as a person and reject me.

It's all the same fear. It just took a different form. My fear defined who I was, and without it, I wasn't enough.

See a fear for what it is. Know that it is just the ego looking to find validation through circumstances and trying to make itself strong.

Allowing your mind to give energy and validity to a feeling that comes from being unconscious only grows more fear.

Laugh it off. Let it go. And place your energy—so much energy!—elsewhere.

Lesson 17 | SURRENDER: Surrender is Freedom

Let me *enlighten* you about the freedom of surrender. It tastes better than the cold glass of Pinot that I am sipping on, sitting at a restaurant in the French Riviera, writing, watching the Euro Cup semi-finals. Surrender is *that* sexy.

It also has no hangover, fucking bonus, right?

Kindergarten students kick our adult baggage-filled arses at surrendering. They're so present with every sandcastle build, lady beetle hunt, playdough fight and pass the parcel game. They're so present, happy, and accepting. They're enlightened.

Surrender does not mean to be walked over. It simply means to let go of fighting, to release resistance. It means the practice of accepting all for what it is, no forcing and no fighting what is. You are responsible for changing what isn't aligned with your truth; after that, you can accept all that remains.

Working to live in a manner that aligns with you authentically and changing what is not your truth is important. Getting up when you get knocked the fuck down is so very important. Being inspired and invigorated by life is critical, yes, but without fighting against what is. That's delusional and insane. It's how a lot of people live, and it leads to misery most of the time.

Difference strengthens the ego, whether that difference is to be more wrong (shame/guilt) or more right (superiority/pride).

Without distinction, without stories, rightness, or wrongness, the ego is limp and lethargic. It has no hold over you. Loving and accepting yourself and your life means that you can use your mind and it doesn't use itself against you.

Lesson 18 | UNITY: Unconditional Love is Unity, Infinity, and Compassion

Loving unconditionally means embracing these two concepts:

- Nothing lasts forever, and everything lasts forever. Unconditional love is infinite, which is to say that all things in this universe, at any stage, birth, near death, high, and low are all unconditionally loveable and part of an infinite cycle of life.
- Love is a part of the soul's condition. It is not something to be claimed, given, received, or, most of all, taken away.

Unconditional love is not to be confused with allowing people to disrespect your boundaries and values or letting people walk all over you. The concepts above simply allow life to flow as it should, rather than allow non-acceptance get in the road of love.

When someone crosses your boundaries, if they project onto you, if they act in an unconscious way that triggers you, hurts you, or harms you, the concept of unconditional love allows you to say, "Yeah, I've been there and done that also; that part of you is also a part of me". And when someone loves you, brings love to your life with theirs, and sprinkles magic shit everywhere, you can also see, "I have that magic also."

Choose to let unconditional love tear the ego to shreds, and be limitless.

We are all in this together, and so, I have something to share.

A letter from my heart to my heart and yours when you feel like an outcast, alone, and in shame; I have something to share, to help you know that I understand that, at times, compassion, tough love, and understanding are what we really need.

Darling,

I'm not disappointed in you. You don't piss me off or frustrate me.

I don't think you're an idiot, hopeless, or lost. I do not think you're a failure. I don't believe that you were born different from everyone and that's why you keep screwing yourself over. I know, for sure, that you are capable of greatness.

Because I do those things too. You and I are the same. I am imperfect just like you. I have been stuck just like you. I am a fuck-up. I am angry. I am uninspired. I am mean and emotional. I am narcissistic. I am impatient and unkind. I am these things.

The difference between you and me is that I have given myself permission to love myself, no matter what.

Stop shaming your past mistakes. Shame fuels sabotage. It fuels pain and anxiety.

Pick yourself up; dust yourself off; look in the damn mirror, and say, "I love you!" to every little part of your past. That's the only way to begin living a different future.

With love,
Me.

LEAD WITH YOUR HEART, GUIDE WITH YOUR HEAD

"Every child is an artist. The problem is how to remain an artist once he grows up."

—**Pablo Picasso**

INTRO: Your Purpose Finds You

"What is my purpose in life?"

Potentially, life's biggest question and, equally, a mind fuck.

I believe that we all know what our unique purpose is, but we've got too many layers of self-bullshitting covering up our truth.

I have witnessed repeatedly, both for myself and clients, that deep misery and inner despair, depression, insecurities, self-sabotage, and addictions arise within us when we do not live a life that aligns with our deepest purpose. But what is purpose? It's coming; I promise.

Like many of the words in this sphere, purpose is a pretty big concept and a bit outdated. How about we still roll with it and bring some clarity and practicality to it.

Psychologist Dr. Victor Frankl, author of probably the most profound book on purpose that I have ever come across and a total must read, *Man's Search for Meaning*, deduces, after experiencing Nazi prisoner of war camps, that suffering is a consequence of not living on purpose. Frankl created a widely used form of psychotherapy called logo therapy; logos means purpose. It's a form of therapy that helps people in suffering to discover their meaning in life and heal their neurosis.

To have meaning in one's life *is* to live. We all have meaning; we all have purpose, but it is up to us to both discover what that is and live it.

Frankl uses the specific word discover in his book. Like him, I recommend that you first discover the meaning of your life every day. Rather than placing emphasis on purpose as something that you do and how people know you, what if it is just *who you are?*

If a spiritual teacher has ever tried to point you towards a purpose and told you to discover that, live that, and express that, it defeats the point of the being and directs us to doing.

Plus, discovering is an adventure. Discovering purpose in each moment and action, through being you, is a treasure hunt that never ends but that is alive in every moment. There is no goal other than to be. Meaning will never leave you.

Purpose can take many forms. Rather than just one single purpose such as doctor, mother, father, firefighter, lawyer, accountant, personal trainer, and so on, I prefer to teach purpose as a consistent choice in every moment to align your decisions with what is in your heart.

To aid you in finding your meaning, simplify the questions to one question: "What does my heart want?' When you follow that, your meaning will take all different forms and show up. It takes the pressure off a little, right?

Instead of, "What is my purpose in life?" or, "What should I do with my life?"—such big, open-ended, mind fuck questions— "What is it that I love?" is simple. Those 'what should I do with my life' style questions are on another level because most people have guilt and shame around it.

"Shame gremlins," as they are called by Dr. Brené Brown, a shame researcher, and psychologist, stop us from asking ourselves what we need to ask if we are to align with our truth.

What we should ask ourselves is, "What does my heart tell me if I am honest, vulnerable, and even a little embarrassed?"

It's a much simpler question, and it gets you out of the logical part of your brain, which wants to label everything within your purpose, such as, a career, how many people you influence, potential income, degrees, and titles. This, revised, puts you back where you belong, which is in touch with your body, your intuition, and your heart.

That's not to say that you need to drop the business suits or that degrees don't matter. It just pulls down the boundaries and dissolves expectations, which are the two things that screw us up the most. This includes all of our self-imposed should and society-imposed shoulds. Stop fucking subordinating. Who is anyone to say what should be important to you?

What do you love? What have you always loved? What did you obsess over when you still had your training wheels on? What could you do all day and not care too much whether you were paid or if you had a decent meal and roof over your head?

People feel so guilty about what is meaningful to them. Maybe the real question I should ask is, "What are you afraid to do?" or maybe, "What would you be completely embarrassed about if you were to create something and people were to scrutinise it?" Perhaps, "What do you love that makes you feel vulnerable but fulfilled?" Okay, I cannot help myself, of course, "What would you do if you woke up with 1 billion dollars in the bank?" And finally, "What would you do every day if there was no way to show anyone (as in, you can't post it anywhere, and no one would ever know what any of us did, and life was completely private)?" See what you come up with.

This might sound a little confusing; however, it's the things that make us feel the most exposed that are often the things that we want to create, do, and experience. It's just that at some point we convinced ourselves that it didn't measure up to a decent purpose.

Call it what you want; we all have one, a meaning. And the bottom line is this: if you don't start living it, the highlights of your week will be *Game of Thrones*, a sale at the liquor store, and a random shag.

You can never quiet the heart for good.

If we just take the pressure off of who we need to be and what purpose looks like, we would all realise that there is absolutely nothing to be done, while paradoxically, it is of the utmost importance to be you in all that you do so that as many moments as possible are filled with purpose. This is not because you are trying to make your life purposeful but because you have found purpose within, and it naturally explodes and spills into everything that you do.

Fear can smother your intuition and mislead it. Intuition can be suffocated by our shallow everyday addictions, but it will never, ever leave us.

So, we may as well listen to it.

Your intuition is when your soul meets the currency of life within your body and mind. You can feel it.

There is something that Elizabeth Gilbert says in her book, *Big Magic,* and it's about a genius. She talks about us not being geniuses but having a genius, and I resonate deeply with this.

The funniest bit about purpose is that, as far as a doing thing is concerned, life is cyclical. Time doesn't exist. You are never not doing enough; you are never behind; no one is ever better; you are never wrong. It's all a mental perception. You don't need to save the fucking world. Take that weight off your shoulders, and start being yourself. You'll eventually realise that authenticity shines a light to others; it offers them freedom; it reflects their greatness; it allows them to be authentic. The cycle continues. When we try too hard, and when our ego gets in the way of living, we fuck it up. We stress; we angst; we block.

Wake up, and live each day with the intention of having fun, being integral, and being present. That is all you need to do. Wake up, and go to work each day without the pressure of having to create outcomes for people. Take that shit as a bonus.

Our heart, our soul, our purpose, our values, they're all the same thing, and they're aligned with something much greater than ourselves.

We think that our ideas and values are something we own and that we are independent of the bigger picture of the universe.

The ego becomes threatened with the approach of freedom and will sabotage it at all costs.

Ever wonder why trying to find your purpose is so stressful?

Your purpose isn't something that you should find; it is something that you are. Your purpose is encrypted within your soul. The mind is the machine that we can use to steer the ship and act out this purpose.

If your life and the world feel stressful, it's because you have too much head and too little heart. You're looking for your purpose amongst the approval of society.

Your purpose isn't stressful.

Timelines are stressful. The belief that you need to do more because you haven't done enough is what creates stress.

Comparison is insecurity.

Trying to control is anxiety.

And these can all be very deathly drives to shift our self-awareness in this human life, but they're also a reminder to sit the fuck down, to calm your mind, and to get back to your heart.

Draw maps and tables and charts if you like. Soothe your mind's needs to know if you must, but know that you are doing it out of fear and not out of love.

"Love is a better master than duty."

—Albert Einstein

Leading with your heart is following your *telos*, your intuition.

A soul without a mind is a soul not evolving, and a mind without a soul is pure analysis and the mechanics of fear.

It looks like stress, anxiety, insecurities, doubts, and sabotage.

The heart is purpose guided, intuition tapped into, and uses the head only when necessary.

The more you that try to tame your heart, the emptier you will be. And the more that you control, the more you will crave, and the bigger slave that you will become to clinging onto every bit of certainty that you can get. Instant gratification will be your heroin. For an unfulfilled soul, short-term stimulation is its only relief. And the ego runs the show because, as well as an addiction to gratification; an unfulfilled soul cultivates insecurities that deepen the wounds of self-destruction and feed the need for bigger and more frequent fixes.

An unfulfilled soul needs stimulation like a thirsty man needs sea water.

Gratification is all around you, attention for your body, attention for *anything* actually, your job, your weekly income, the label your doctor gave your current psychological status and behaviour, your surname, your gender, your associates, your fame, your boyfriend's surname, your girlfriend's breast size, the number of hours that you work every week, your superannuation, your yoga pose, your 3 million followers, a sugary treat, a hard whisky, that overpriced brand, a big fat problem that you never stop talking about, a crisp wine, a cheesy pizza, an indulgent brownie, a season of *Suits*, or a hierarchical status in the gaming world. It's all part of the rat-race, and it's everywhere.

You must relinquish your need for control and just let it flow. You must listen with the beat of your heart. Stop playing small by living in your head.

Those who speak too loudly have no idea. Those who know to shut up and listen will tune into their intuition. As vulnerable and as terrifying and ridiculously illogical as it might sometimes seem, you must give up the mind games if you want success, freedom, fullness, richness, and joy in your life.

Use your brain when you need it. Be grateful for the gift of your mind, and use it to focus on what you want to create and what you already know that you are capable of but are too afraid of not getting or giving up or being rejected if you become successful at. Those fears make you screw yourself over and play small.

Other than that, have the courage to seek deeper meaning in your life. Have guts. Do yourself the justice. You deserve it. You are born to be true to you, so listen to your heart.

Lesson

19 | LIVE: Your Purpose is to Know Yourself and Live Yourself, Fear and All

Purpose: To be you. To most, those are the scariest words that they've ever read. They've spent most of their lives in a relationship with a false identity that has always said how they are not good enough or that nothing will measure up to the best of the best, so they may as well just colour between the lines and play it safe.

Fuck that shit.

You, me, and any person, at any moment in our time, have a purpose that is forever in motion, forever transforming, and forever flowing through life. Your ability to connect to a purpose in this world, something external, is directly proportionate to the extent of connection that you have with the authentic depths of your soul and intuition. It's a timeless, in motion, constant state of listening beyond thinking and being disciplined and brave enough to stand up to the voice in your head and say, "Who I am and what I must give by being me is certainly enough."

We use age, money, and time to justify ignoring our deepest inner values and not living them, but the real reason that we ignore our values is the fear of rejection and failure, and, most of all, the fear of letting go of all of your excuses and owning the fact that you, yes you, are fucking amazing.

"You may be 38 years old, as I happen to be. And one day, some great opportunity stands before you and calls you to stand up for some great principle, some great issue, some great cause.

"And you refuse to do it because you are afraid. You refuse to do it because you want to live longer. You're afraid that you will lose your job, or you are afraid that you will be criticized, or that you will lose your popularity, or you're afraid that somebody will stab you, or shoot at you, or bomb your house; so, you refuse to take the stand.

> "Well, you may go on and live until you are 90, but you're just as dead at 38 as you would be at 90. And the cessation of breathing in your life is but the belated announcement of an earlier death of the spirit."
>
> **—Martin Luther King Jr.**

If you don't know who you are, how will you live your purpose? And if you don't live your purpose, don't expect to spend too many days being able to look up at the sun, or at a flower in a garden, or a great mountain range and find beauty and fulfilment in them. You will be too busy searching for meaning and the cause of the emptiness in your soul.

Being us is the only thing that we need to do in this lifetime. The only fucking thing that is important is never conforming to the image of who and what we believe we need to be, but instead, doing the work that it takes to peel back those layers, shatter the masks, shed the conditions of the mind, and discover who it is that we are. Then, we can live it.

Lesson 20

PRACTICE: Leading With Your Heart is a Constant Practice of Connection

Tolle wrote,

> *"Your life has an inner purpose and an outer purpose. Inner purpose concerns being and is primary. Outer purpose concerns doing, and it is secondary. Your inner purpose is to awaken. It is as simple as that. You share that purpose with every other person on the planet— because it is the purpose of humanity. Your inner purpose is an essential part of the purpose of the whole, the universe and its emerging intelligence. Your outer purpose can change over time. It varies greatly from person to person. Finding and living in alignment with the inner purpose is the foundation for fulfilling your outer purpose. It is the basis for true success. Without that alignment, you can still achieve certain things through effort, struggle, determination, and sheer hard work or cunning. But there is no joy in such endeavour, and it invariably ends in some form of suffering."*

—Eckhart Tolle, *The Power of Now*

You know what happened when I decided to follow my purpose? I ended up in the hospital. Yep. When I quit radiation therapy and studied human behaviour and ran my first retreat, I spent almost a week In the hospital after it for acute kidney and liver failure. My friend cortisol and I spent way too much time together, and eventually, my nervous system said, "Screw you, Amber; you're going on your arse" My liver and kidneys couldn't process the toxins from stress and, probably, a heavily imbalanced diet of coffee and lack of food. I collapsed and called myself an ambulance the day after I got home from the retreat. I followed my heart, and I worked more hours; I earned less; I ignored my health, and I was being stressed out of my mind. I had no time for loving relationships or friends, and I probably would have been a lot worse off without the 5 to 6 Bikram classes, which then served as both a saviour and an escape for the first 18 months of following my heart.

Why am I telling you this? I want you to understand that I know firsthand that even when we lead with our heart, we can still be disconnected and out of balance. Your head can get in the road, especially when you are fresh into the unknown, and create all sorts of havoc. However, by always remembering your primary purpose and coming back home to you, you can cultivate connection, peace, inspiration, stillness, and reduce some of the complete freakouts and meltdowns that come with extending your comfort zone, which has been chaining you down for so long.

Doing what you love doesn't equate to no stress. It's doing what we love and still taking fear with us that can make it stressful.

In fact, there are boundless amounts of potential stress in doing what you love when you are disconnected. Connection directly links up to purpose, because our purpose is living our values, and our values are etched into our soul, and our soul is intertwined into this authentic, imperfect human experience. When we first begin to take some leaps into fear, we're yet to master the discomfort of the unknown and stress, anxiety, and overwhelm can kick in quite easily.

Just like going without oxygen for a few minutes can cause extreme physical breakdown, going without connection for moments can start the spiral of emotional and spiritual stress.

Therefore, reconnection through awareness of the difference between your jabbering mind and who you are is of the utmost importance.

The bottom line is that we are human. We want things to be in our control; we want to be able to predict, feel safe, and find certainty. The only certain thing about following your heart is that there is very little control and a shitload of the unknown. So practically speaking, it amounts to a hell of a lot of courage, persistence, and willingness to move through the human emotions of fear, doubt, failure, insecurities, resistance, stress, anxiety, and overwhelm. Do NOT get caught in the self-help bullshit about your purpose being so fulfilling that you'll never be stressed.

Purpose and discomfort go hand in hand. Being comfortable would probably mean that you are erring too far on the side of safety, staying just within your limits, and in the safe zone of what you know.

It's a no from me. Why? Because if we are not stretching ourselves, then we are sitting stagnant. And this is a constant world of energy in motion. If we try to sit still, stay in our shells, and get too comfortable, we are almost guaranteed to find ourselves wanting to dip our toes in unhealthy stimulation soon enough.

Being on purpose is a two-birds-one-stone practice. When you are aligned with your truth, which you can only hear when the mind is still, and you are present, you will be connected *and* live authentically. It may sound like a chicken-or-egg situation, but let's dive down a little. Does being present come first or being on purpose? The answer is, of course, connection, or consciousness. Because of all three—presence, purpose, connectedness—are one and the same.

When you go into the big wide world of the unknown and begin to chip away at how you used to be and what you used to do and finally find your nerve, always remember, uncertainty, discomfort, unease, fear, anxiety, and stress are going to be coming along for the ride, and this is perfectly okay. You don't even have to know what you are doing. Sometimes, you must realise that the risk of staying comfortable, in what is safe but not happy, is far worse than the discomfort of facing the unknown. Fear expands the size of the risk and stress to become much bigger than it is. And the longer and more frequently that we think about it, the bigger the porky pie lie about how scary and difficult the task of diving into uncertainty becomes. Sometimes, you just have to throw your hands up and say, "Fuck it. Let's go!"

For example, two very talented and inspiring friends of mine, Carla and Emma Pappas, decided to ditch the corporate life to quite literally *follow their bliss*. Their business, *The Merrymaker Sisters*, provides some of the yummiest and healthiest recipes and positive goodness, and it is booming since they decided to dive head first into fear. It came with a ton of hard work, but the key ingredient was choosing to make their days consist of something that lit them up, something that came from deep within and that was worth the struggle, the uncertainty, and the stress. Most of all, they moved through fear for. They left with no plan, no savings, and no idea how to run a business, and they didn't even tell their parents that they quit their jobs! They embody what it means to be unfuckwithable on every level and are a perfect example of their outer purpose, the business, showing up as they moved forward just being them, *merry and blissful.*

On the flip side, purpose can be expressed and explored in the very job or role that you have right now. You don't need to necessarily quit what you are you doing and go live from a laptop because, perhaps, all that you need is to change your perspective about what you do and to be able to see how it already connects you to your values. Perhaps, you need to step up and start expressing yourself more, and that's when meaning will find you.

Maybe you are the best damn accountant, electrician, teacher, parent, ice-cream scooper, or garbage truck driver that there is, and your job allows you to express yourself fully. Maybe you can disrupt and shake the rigid culture of where you are by just being you. Maybe it's your purpose to be so untamable in who you are in the job or company that you're in that you transform an entire industry or at least the immediate circle you touch. That is powerful and should not be dismissed or underestimated. It's not the quantity but quality that matters here.

A perfect example of someone who is doing this is my friend, Clarissa Rawyward. Clarissa is an amazing divorce lawyer who wrote, *Happy Lawyer, Happy Life*. Her innovative ideas and approach to a very regimented culture are impacting not just the lives of the families she assists through their divorce but also lawyers around the world.

Finally, if there isn't a job that you feel enables you to be fully you, create one of your own. Just like my brother from another mother, Ronsley Vaz, has done. Ronsley is the author of the book, *Amplify*, and the owner and director of one of the most successful audio agencies on the planet also called Amplify. Additionally, he is the founder of the event *We Are Podcast*, which is the second biggest podcasting conference in the world. When I asked him where he got the idea for the event from, he simply said, "Well, I really wanted an event like this, but it didn't exist, so I created it." And that's that.

Don't get me wrong, if you are in a 9-5 that you fucking hate, a relationship that doesn't make you feel expansive and free, a country, town or city that tires you, a routine that's just what you have always done, or a mindset that says, "This is just how it is," please very carefully consider getting the fuck out.

It doesn't have to be right now, but you can decide right now to start making an action plan to change it. If that's you, do not read any further. Get out a pen and paper, and write down the next three steps that you can take to make a change. And if you don't know, call someone who does; message someone who has done what you want to do. Trust me when I say that if you reach out to someone who has followed their heart, they'd be more than happy to have a quick chat or even a coffee and help you out. People who know the freedom of breaking free want others to feel the same.

Lesson 21

HUMBLE: Remain Humble in Authenticity and Your Purpose Will Emerge

When I first started working in personal development and saw, "Live your dreams," "Follow your heart," or "Break free, and discover your purpose," on my Facebook feed or my email inbox, I would get excited. I would think about how beautiful it was that more people were encouraging a freer way of life. Now, five years deep, every time I see something similar, my sarcasm kicks in to deal as sadness churns within me. It sends people into a spiral of anxiety and self-doubt. "What is my purpose?"

This glorified "find our purpose" bullshit is what keeps us stuck.

I am calling total and utter bullshit. You know your purpose. This insidious excuse of needing to know what your purpose is to be happy is killing people, and it's destroying lives. You do not need to leave your job. You cannot expedite self-discovery because purpose, passion, and impermanence are intertwined, and if you try to box it up into one career, one job, or one role, you're skipping out on life. It's an ever-unfolding discovery of both finding meaning and purpose and just being you all rolled into one. What you do just happens as a natural, secondary action because you know who you are and you make both intuitive and logical decisions from an empowered place. Your purpose just kind of shows up when you stop worrying about what it is.

You've totally got to get down and dirty with yourself to uncover and discover what your external purpose looks like.

"We fear to discover that we are more than we think we are. More than our parents/children/teachers think we are. We fear that we actually possess the talent that our still, small voice tells us, that we actually have the guts, the perseverance, the capacity. We fear that we truly can steer our ship, plant our flag, reach our Promised Land. We fear this because, if it's true, then we become estranged from all we know. We pass through a membrane. We become monsters and monstrous."

—Steven Pressfield, *The War of Art: Break Through the Blocks & Win Your Inner Creative Battles*

Not a single person was born a blank canvas waiting to be painted into this person or that person by the opinions of the world. We are born possessing a fertile and highly unique soul. This means that while we always have freedom of choice, we don't have unlimited choices in our purpose.

In fact, we can't just be whatever we want because not everything will fulfill us. It's our task to discover the specific destiny that our soul chose before it entered this world.

Our job is not to chip away our individuality until we are the perfect cut-out of success but to dig into ourselves, find who we are, and become it. This is a terrifying quest. We are all afraid of our magnificence as we hide behind fear and shame. The moment when we own it, we must leave behind all of the excuses that allowed us to take the easy path. This is to say, what you fear is not failure, it's your very own success.

By "know yourself", I'm talking here about being connected with yourself and then living through this space of connectedness. A life of meaning, giving, and contribution—not in a martyr, sacrificial sense—will bring about a fulfilment of the intrinsic desire that we all have to give to another. Through generosity, we receive joy. To be on purpose is a dual act of staying connected and externally living life from your heart. It means aligning with your values, truth, and authentic inspiration and creating a life from this. Your outer purpose is to transfer your inner purpose of *being* into outwardly doing and expressing your unique individual soul.

My purpose is my fuel. I know what it is, and I use it. I am born to teach people to strip away the parts of life that are not exactly what their heart finds true and meaningful.

You must own your purpose and then live it too. Again, this is simple but not easy. But what if you stopped putting a label on it—a career or a role or a certificate—and just did what fired up your soul? What if you did the thing that gives you life and meaning?

Let this philosophy creep into every crevice of your being.

In the Tao Te Ching, Lao Tzu said, "Knowing others is intelligence; knowing yourself is true wisdom. Mastering others is strength; mastering yourself is true power." I believe that what he is talking about is overcoming fear within yourself and being authentic in every aspect of your being and doing. He is talking about living on purpose.

Jim Carrey is an excellent example of being conscious of the ego and using it to fulfil his purpose. His incredible wit, which requires his mind and requires thinking, brings joy to millions. When you watch and listen to him, his humour has to ability to pull you out of thought and into complete connection. You are conscious. He is an example of an ego existing and being utilised to bring about consciousness. And as an extension of the first (inner) purpose of being conscious, he is also expressing and creating, through his doing, the second (outer) purpose of him being a captivating actor.

It is awareness and intention that make the difference.

"Accomplish but do not boast, accomplish without show, accomplish without arrogance, accomplish without grabbing, accomplish without forcing."

—Lao Tzu

Lesson 22 | OTHERS: People's Fear Will Try to Pull You Down, so Love Them Anyway, and Pull Them Up

I was on Facebook scrolling through some posts recently, and I saw a friend had shared one of my posts. Someone wound up commenting on it that I was a narcissist. Woah!

Instantly, I felt sick. Immediately, I scanned the post for hints of obsessive, self-righteousness manipulations and carelessness for others. I could find nothing. Exhale. Confusion now came over me. *What could they possibly be referring to?* And then I smiled and relaxed. I remembered the words that had come out of my mouth only a few days earlier when I was speaking with a client who was having some issues with a friend.

My client's friend had told him that she thought that his "new, weird behaviour" of earlier nights, exercise, and working on his new business showed off how much better he thought that he was than everybody else. The friend had called my client a "new-age, boring faggot" and asked him to call her when he grew his balls back. Ouch!

They'd been friends since kindergarten. And understandably, my client felt a disheartened.

I replied, *"Darling, never dull your light because it shines in someone's eyes. It's like this: when someone who's living a life that they're not deep-down satisfied with sees you doing what makes you happy and successful, they will attack you because the pain that they feel inside of themselves is unbearable. Your authenticity triggers them. Of course, it's not their intention to hurt. And that's why we respond with love. What feels like daggers coming into your heart from them is just their pain spilling out of their mouth. Love them. Thank them for reflecting to you the part of yourself that you have let go. Then keep doing shit that makes you happy."*

Never sacrifice your fulfilment for another person's acceptance, even if it's your best friend. Unfortunately, it's what I see most of society do every single day; the same old patterns repeat. The same old standard of a good and acceptable life is sought. Fuck good, and screw acceptable. You deserve *incredible*.

I see people mistake self-awareness, self-love, authenticity, and boundaries for narcissism every single day, including the occasion when my friend's friend questioned me on Facebook and when I was coaching my client who's friend questioned him.

We've been boxed in for so long. Shred up the box! Instead, build a ship to carry your heart's desires into the world, and create a meaningful life.

People fear their greatness, and they will challenge yours until they have owned theirs. Don't let it pull you back; let it drive you forward.

> *"Be careful what you water your dreams with. Water them with worry and fear, and you will produce weeds that choke the life from your dream. Water them with optimism and solutions, and you will cultivate success. Always be on the lookout for ways to turn a problem into an opportunity for success. Always be on the lookout for ways to nurture your dream."*
>
> **—Lao Tzu**

Love yourself. You are worth it, and so are they.

CODE FOUR

GET CONNECTED

INTRO: Connection is The GO GO Juice of Being Unfuckwithable

Moving forward, you'll see, read, and feel a different part of Amber that peeks her head out when I start talking about connection. It's a littler, warmer, and fuzzier than the one at the beginning of the book, who is pissed off at us wasting our potential.

Holy fuck, we are here. The core of the solution to the world's misery. *happy dance* Feel free to quote me on that. I will bet my bottom dollar that in 100 years, or even sooner, that meditation and connection will be a part of every school, medical system, and everyday household practice.

Connection is a decision. It's a choice. It's a practice. It's our teacher, the test and the answer all in one.

When we have the courage to reach into the soul of the world and find that it is the same stuff that makes up our soul, we see the reflection of ourselves within this inception, and we can create miracles.

Here is what you need to know about connection, meditation, focus, and presence.

All of the quotes about entire oceans being in a drop, that love is always the answer, and that we always have everything we need can be experienced by the very simple and straightforward practice of connection, rather than just a poetic sounding concept on a Pinterest board.

Connection is like the current that holds the potential power to make a light bulb glow. It's always accessible to us, even in the darkest moments, in times of stress, insecurities, rage, addiction and impulse. Connection is waiting patiently, asking nothing at all, and ready to give a current. Connection is always available to bring light into our lives.

There is a particular moment during a TEDx talk by Johann Hari, a researcher who wrote *Chasing the Scream: The First and Last Days of the War on Drugs* when he says, "The core of the problems [of addiction] is not being able to bear to be present in your life."

It's so fucking sexy, seriously. When researching for this book, I found Hari's work and felt a hum of YES in my system. I realised that everything I suspected and researched about the connection between inauthenticity and suffering, and connection and fulfilment, had all been studied and validated by this incredible man.

Now, he talks about connection primarily between humans.

While I encourage people to connect with others, especially those who are on the same wavelength (pun intended), I want primarily to encourage an invincible connection with yourself. This connection with yourself makes you instantly and constantly in power. Connection with our self never leaves; it's us that abandons ourselves and then searches for connection at the bottom of a bottle, dollar bill, or one-night stand.

We must learn how to flick the switch to turn on the current.

The Rise of Superman by Steve Kotler is a book about, what he refers to as, a flow state accessed instantly for extreme sports athletes. Due to the high-risk nature of sports like rock climbing, skydiving, and surfing, our conscious awareness switches into a state of being that supersedes thinking, memory, skill, talent, and instinct. It's the pure state of presence, centered-being, and oneness as opposed to the limited mental perspective of dualities.

When we forget our soul, which sometimes I call home, it's like constantly wearing shitty tasting beer goggles called duality. Alas, all things according to the ego are either something to be feared and resisted or to be wanted and desired.

The trouble with the ego is that when left unchecked and identified with as us, it demolishes our self-worth and happiness into smithereens through its natural process of comparison. It can be a cunning, little shit, always wanting to stay alive and, thus, always coming up with ways to keep us thinking. For examples, it creates problems and gives us the worst-case scenarios or tells us that to do more, etc. I don't blame it; I'd be terrified as well if I realised that all I had to do to disappear was to stop thinking.

You will never hear me suggest to get rid of the ego or blame it. I know, I know, I take little stabs at in facetiously to make a point; however, it's important to understand that making this concept something to resist is the concept of the ego itself in play.

The ego is our thoughts; it's our responsibility to realise that it's not who we are. Blaming the ego is like blaming our ignorance. Instead, I suggest wearing the ego as a shawl. Let it play its role in life, but don't get to the point where the shawl is wrapped so tightly around your neck that you don't know where you begin and where the shawl ends, where all you experience is asphyxiation, separate from pure joy, love, and authenticity. Do not let it become suffocation through identification. The ego keeps us evolving as it lures us into suffering, but we can use it to become empowered and self-aware as we let go of it. It exists for us to chip away at it until all that's left is us, the soul. How far away is your phone right now? I bet it's within a meter, or you know exactly where it is. We've replaced true connection with ourselves with a connection to a bunch of profiles putting their 10/10 life forward.

The head will have all sorts of excuses about why meditation, creativity, connection with our intrinsic values, and authentic purpose and doing things that we love are all a waste of time. Of course, to keep itself alive, the mind will have a story about how hard it is, how there are so many things to do. To the mind, there is always a back ache to adjust for, an itch to scratch, dishes to clean, bills to pay, weight to lose, failures to reflect on, or the future to worry about. You *must* realise that this is how connection is our test.

The bad news is that there is still no magic pill. It's simple and effortless, but we have been so utterly conditioned to look for problems, complex solutions, and analyse endlessly while functioning in a society that equates working hard with success. I have mused plenty of times at the irony of the simplest solutions that are often ignored. There is a connection between our sense of identities, the ego feeding fear, problems, feeling so unsatisfied with life, the Western world's inability to stop and think for a moment, and our refusal accept that the antidote to the emptiness inside exists right here and now.

Have you ever stood on a beach, watching the currents pulling around 70% of Earth's surface, breaking upon each other? The waves roll this way and that while all the animals in the ocean work with the flow. They use it and live harmoniously within, and you suddenly know all there is to know about life?

Our impulse and addictive habits reflect our lack of connection, be it in each moment or life overall. Through being able not to react and give life over to excuses, justifications, and resistance we use our connection. And it gives us all the answers to life, through allowing us to stop searching for answers and start being.

Just as connection can happen in a moment, so can disconnection. If for just a moment you listen to fear, an impulse can rise within you.

Also, before you start turning your life inside out and upside down, take a breath.

Focus on shifting your focus before you change your career that isn't making you fulfilled. If you start from trying to change the outside without working within first, it will end up a fucking hot mess of stress. It will be much more beneficial to work on your moment-to-moment connection and cultivate positive work and habits into your life. The courage to be yourself and make those big massive changes like career and relationships will just show up.

We need to stop underestimating the greatness of doing absolutely nothing. There is greatness in not working hard or hustling but just being, be it for 10 minutes a day or an hour a day. Start somewhere; start where you can; start now. There is great value in seeing everything and not having to look, in hearing everything and not having to listen, and in feeling the temptation of doing and not having to do. All this time, the antidote has been right here, but we haven't been still enough to see it.

Connection is so very simple,
so very effortless.

Like most solutions to the greatest problems on this planet, connection is so simple.

It is the most underestimated antidepressant and anti-anxiety medication, emotional healer, PTSD manager, and addiction treatment available. There are countless studies of meditation and mindfulness being used to treat neurosis and medically diagnosed illnesses and addictions, with reports of increased cultivated joy, inspiration, happiness, and confidence.

Let's liken a gun to the process of disconnection.

The trigger on the gun is the potential of stimulus waiting to be indulged in, for example, the available sex, the pull of Facebook feeds, the scent of sugar, or the lure of wine. What fires the shot is us giving into the impulse or temptation. The bullet is the choice of stimuli, the 7Fs for which we indulge in, and it hits us, deep in our soul. Each time, we take another hit, we sever the connection to our authentic self and become more reliant on the stimuli to keep us satisfied.

Connection, meditation, presence, being, the now, love, essence, energy, universe, and even God, are all pointing, like a compass, to the same thing. A place that I like to call home. It's where we all sit on our common ground. And while connection won't always look like a BBQ at the beach, you will always have the ability to connect to you to home.

Connection brings you to a space of authenticity, from which all choices emanate an empowered, confident, grounded, and magnetic energy. Connection helps you tap into a sweet spot where life isn't lived through memory, but through curiosity, freedom and inspiration.

Connection to purpose, which, remember, is who you authentically are and what your unique and incredible soul desires

Connection to relationships with yourself, others, and the world around you that are from a place of unconditional love

- Connection to your emotions
- Connection to your intuition, soul, and unique wilderness
- Connection to joy, fun, creativity, and exploration
- Connection to breath
- Connection to the present moment
- Connection to nature
- Connection to life itself

Lesson 23

CONSCIOUSNESS: Don't "Know it," Experience it

It is time to try and describe the indescribable.

What is indescribable? Well, here it goes.

The word consciousness is a noun. A noun is a naming word for those who forgot their second-grade English (like me). Nouns serve as a label or name for something, but this word, consciousness, is meant to be pointing towards, umm, how do I put this? Nothing. As soon as we assign a name to it, it's a something. It's not nothing anymore.

Hence, it is indescribable.

All spiritual texts sound like fucking riddles, and this is why! They use metaphors because there is nothing to describe consciousness, nothingness, or mystery.

More than likely, you have heard people reference being in the now. Clichés like this used to annoy me until I realised that it was just my projection of myself, wanting to be more important and above the clichés. I used to think that it was ridiculous, you know, these ideas like a "flowing of consciousness?" What the fuck, right?

My mind also wanted to fight the concept of consciousness, like, *"Really? That's where we came from? A bunch of infinite energy that grows and collapses itself repeatedly?"*

However, the more that I dug, observed myself and my mind, and looked for holes in the concept, the more I was met with the overwhelming truth that these great scientists, spiritual teachers, inventors, and artists, the ones who all came to the same conclusion were correct. *Ah, fuck it. The clichés are true.*

If ya can't beat 'em, join 'em; right?

It took a lot of my self-enquiry to experience, at last, the same deep awesomeness that all of those others realised we can tap into. I use the word connection instead of consciousness because I find that the understanding of connection is cleaner and simpler, like a switch that we can flick on or off. Most people are flicked to disconnected. It becomes so habitual that we don't even know it. And this disconnection causes unnecessary angst in our lives, such as

- Being disconnected from our emotions means that we're unable to be vulnerable, and we have difficulty forming healthy relationships with our self, others, and the world around us. We are ignorant that vulnerability is a strength.
- Being disconnected from self-awareness means that we're in denial of the human nature that says we are **all** fucked up.
- Being disconnected from purpose means searching for a self-serving and self-absorbed validation stemming from the ever-lacking sense of self, which is devised by the mind.

We are idiots, always busy chasing validation and rainbows! When we're disconnected from life, we're never present right now.

Cue another old cliché; "There is no time, only now." Honestly, though, it's true; there isn't! The past and the future are just memories and imagination. It's all brain work. It doesn't exist until it arrives. It doesn't exist now that it has passed. So, when you are disconnected from the now, you never arrive in your life.

I found this awesome reference in one of Mark Manson's articles called *This is Water*. He shares a commencement speech made by one of this favourite authors. I found it to be a simple yet profound explanation of what is hidden in plain sight; consciousness is everywhere and nowhere. You may prefer to think of it as continuous, infinite energy that expands on itself. This is just another way of conceptualising something that, once conceptualised, is already misunderstood.

Two young fish are swimming along when they happen to meet an older fish swimming the other way. The older fish nods at them and says, "Morning, boys. How's the water?" The two, young fish continue swimming for a while until one of them looks over to the other and says, "What the hell is water?"

Connection is the water. It is already available to us. It's here. It always has been, and it always will be.

Disconnection is the fish. If the fish says, "Shit, I'm so thirsty. I wish I had some water" that would be disconnected because the fish is looking for something it exists in.

Disconnection is living in the past or the future.

What I learned is that I gained back all the energy that I had been spending on unconsciously focusing on validation and upholding my imagined identity, which let me tell you was a shit ton.

Practically speaking, a lot of our general suffering is created through expectation. When you authentically create from a place of non-thought, there is no expectation, and the result is a product of flow. And since most people avoid creativity to avoid the vulnerability of rejection and failure, in authentic creativity the fear is not there, and the quality of the work is almost always better.

I've pretty much located what is commonly named intuition in a flow state, or *genuine soul space*.

Personally, what I like best about life coming from intuition is how much you just trust it without worries or fear. There is a lack of attachment to outcomes and deadlines.

Imagine never struggling with not knowing what to do ever again, because you are always plugged into your intuition. This is one of the many, many pros to tuning into your intuition. All of the clichés about happiness come when you stop searching for it. Happiness is here where consciousness comes in. Also, here is courage through vulnerability. Also, here is decreasing depression, anxiety, PTSD, guilt, shame, and neurosis. Here, as well, is fearlessness. Here is no doubt; here is all of it. It all begins with connection, effortlessness connection.

So, want to come?

Lesson
24 | NOTHINGNESS: The Bliss of Doing Absolutely Nothing

Here is a great paradox; doing nothing is best spent doing something that we can do.

Meditate, for fuck sake, whatever that looks like for you.

When we stop, it can seem like, to the part of us who always needs to be busy, the world is passing you by.

But the truth is, when you don't stop, it's you that passes through life without ever really living.

Remember the whole path of least resistance bullshit that the mind wants to take? Meditation is the opposite of resistance because it's focused. Focused means not following thoughts around you like they mean something important; therefore, you will experience resistance in traditional meditation that looks and sounds like a bunch of important things that need doing.

I wanted to give you an actual meditation to do, so if you head to my website, www.amberhawken.com/tulmeditation, you'll see a Book Resources section that includes a guided meditation.

Help to stop the glorification of busy as one of the greatest slogans that our present culture can stand behind because our constant compulsion to be busy stems from an insecure place that isn't serving us. If you are busy to the point of exhaustion, your body will give you feedback, and you should listen.

How often do we just get busier so we can feel like we are something or someone?

Doing nothing is the opposite of this because doing nothing isn't really doing nothing at all.

Doing nothing looks like lying in bed in the dark and simply being.

Doing nothing looks like going out in nature and taking it all in.

When we are doing nothing, we're giving a trusting hug to our soul and honouring that we are perfect just the way we are.

This is the true meaning of trust.

You see, we don't need to run a marathon, raise money for a cause, or start a new school training program to prove to ourselves that we are an okay person.

I mean, maybe we want to do some of these things, and that's great, but if we think doing more activities is going to get us where we want to go, it is very possible that we are missing the point.

Our systems are wise, most likely wiser than we could ever fathom. Our days are busy; this is the reality of being human in the 21st century. Our days are filled with stress, responsibility, worry, and choices. Most of us are living with system overload all of the time.

Doing nothing is the best way to unwind and unravel all the information that easily becomes toxic junk in our systems.

Doing nothing can be quite difficult. It can also be anxiety-provoking.

When we stop, turn off our screens, put away our to-do lists, and cancel our social plans, what we are left with is *ourselves*. And we often feel a sense of inadequacy so deep that we would do anything to run toward busyness again.

This is when we must come back to the amazing paradox of nothingness. It is in doing nothing that this anxiety can unwind itself.

The anxiety comes from the story that we are only okay when we are busy, and, thus, being busy becomes a way to escape the anxiety. This story is a lie, but our system doesn't know this story is a lie because it has been told this story so many times.

The nothingness itself will heal this sense of inadequacy.

Under the anxiety are power, trust, faith, stillness, and a big heart ready to share love.

This can be hard to believe, but it is only hard because we haven't taken the time to experience this truth.

If we are spinning with worry, doubting our choices, feeling unsure about who we are and what we are truly supposed to do on this planet, there is one choice that will bring the answers every time.

Get quiet.

Do nothing.

Have no expectations, except to be brave and courageous; stop all the busy spinning, and just be with your essence for a little while.

Often, the simplest solutions are the most effective. The challenge is that they can seem too simple to the ego for us to believe that they are going to work.

We think more research, more emails, and more planning and scheming will fix our lives, but the answers that we are looking for aren't outside of us. Everything that we need is already in our being.

We just need to stop,

listen,

get quiet,

do nothing.

Just be, and let the beautiful truth of our loving hearts emerge.

Lesson

25 | A DROP: Connection and Basic Physics

If I can give you any advice to speed up this process and make it less painful, it's this; *let go of your need to know*. The urge to know can still exist, but don't let it take you down a path of confusion and fear.

And know this:

You already have the answers; your brain just hasn't caught up yet.

The following explanation of consciousness has been constructed from a presentation by Dr. John Demartini.

Consciousness is the highest frequency and the smallest wavelength in existence.

The highest frequency is called the Planck length. Everything that manifests in this world is built from a multiple of this— you, me, everything that exists. It's one common unit, oneness. At Planck length, there is no distinction between any of us.

If you're wondering why there are so many quotes about us being a drop in the ocean and the whole ocean in a drop, it's because we are. It's spaceless, timeless, massless, and changeless at this frequency. It occupies no space or time, and it is the essence of our existence. It has no condition. It is unconditional.

The word energy is made up of the Latin "en" meaning "being" and "er" meaning "force." Energy is another name for spirit.

John Archibald Wheeler, along with a bunch of other ancient gurus, artists, and philosophers, described the universe as a being made of love. If we are steady and we have love, we see things as both-sided simultaneously. And he came up with a nicely fitting acronym for SOUL: Spirit Of Unconditional Love.

Another way of understanding all of this is to imagine a spinning top, half is black, and half is white. If it spins at an infinite speed, it will stand tall instead of toppling over, and it will appear grey instead of black and white. It will be one. As the frequency slows, it will wobble, and we will see the black and white separateness again.

Our consciousness is like that spinning top. It can either be steady or unsteady, in a state of equilibrium or a state of instability.

When we hold our frequency at a high state through our actions, our presence, and thoughts, we are steady within ourselves; one could say, we are connected and consciously aware, coming from a place of non-judgment or wholeness where we see things as they are, not as a one-sided perspective. The vibrational frequency is so fast that gravity doesn't hold it. It stands straight, and it is certain, like intuition. When you vibrate at a high frequency, you are coming from intuition.

If we lower our vibrational frequency, we become *unstable* and heavy. We drop into a state of non-equilibrium and lose awareness. Eventually, we slow down so much that we drop into a state of duality, seeing things as black and white. Our perspective is no longer whole. It is filtered through a judgment process, which is fear via the ego. We wobble and become unsteady. We wobble, and our shadow aspects arise. The dual nature of being human and having both negative and positive sides becomes apparent. This is the journey of a soul: to come into human form and then rise back into consciousness.

As our frequency slows, we return to our emotional baggage as everything goes through a categorisation of one or the other, positive or negative, black or white. Nothing is recognised as whole at this level, at the state of the human ego, which is a slower vibrational frequency.

Expressions like "infinite expansiveness," and words like "energy," "light," "love," and "freedom" are used to describe soul and consciousness by many spiritual teachers without such an explanation as you are about to read here. I believe that this is because these are simply the words that describe what they felt or experienced when they dropped into non-thought. These spiritual teachers may have just relinquished control of the how, surrendering and not needing an explanation, unlike I did.

Fear is what always stands between you and what you want.

- *Fear of failure*
- *Fear of not being loved*
- *Fear of not being enough*
- *Fear of success*
- *Fear of the new*
- *Fear of uncertainty*
- *Fear of the uncontrollable*
- *Fear of control*

When you have connection, when you are conscious, the place where you come from your soul and through intuition, there is no fear.

"To a mind that is still, the whole universe surrenders."

—Lao Tzu

When I read the above quote, I feel a softness sweep over me. I want to tell you; *begin to allow.* Let the natural state of your soul come out of you in this life. Live with genuine authenticity, and find yourself at higher frequencies. Quit believing that you need to *do* something; life will emerge as you let it happen. Stop trying to force anything.

How do you stop forcing? You just allow. If you feel your mind trying to analyse or if you feel the ego sneak in, judging, and resisting life through its opinions and attachments, let it be. Watch how it does that. And as you watch, instead of running the story, your true sense of self will just pop up like a daisy.

That constant need to hold on, it's not really you. Knowing this is all you need to begin and all you will ever really need.

Lesson 26 | INTUITION: Your Quiet and Constant Voice

Your soul is always singing to the universe, asking it to bring you what you need so that you can see what to do next. The screwed-up thing is that we no longer listen. We talk way too much. We know so much that we are idiots. We look to the past for answers. We want validation, certainty, and security.

Any logical person would concur that when the boat is moving with the stream, the time it takes to ride to the destination will be shorter than if the boat is moving against the current. If the boat has gone against the flow, however, the waves, the crashing, and the rough rise can add not only excessive hours to the journey but also excessive chaos and turbulence.

The question is; do you want to flow or do you want to fight? This is the difference between following your intuition and resisting it.

Many of us are raised to believe that logic is the best way to decide, weighing the pros and cons back and forth. The truth is, though, life is illogical.

We plan for one thing, and the opposite happens. We get upset and disappointed because, somehow, we believed that we had control over how each step would go, especially when we mapped it out so logically.

Intuition is always in operation 24/7. It nudges us in the direction that we should go. It is uncomplicated, contrary to our logical belief that we must analyse everything to the *nth* degree. It's our internal map, our friendly guide.

The brain operates from our experience. Intuition operates from our truth. We always know the truth, but we let past experiences interfere with our journey, to keep us safe. Our mind is an encyclopedia of past experiences, always drawing upon itself for information. This can keep us repeating patterns or abstaining from risk because of the fear that the same thing will happen to us again. Intuition, on the other hand, knows no time. It is not looking at the past as a barometer for what will happen in the future. If something didn't work out in the past, intuition doesn't care. There is an opportunity for different circumstances, people, and outcomes than there was last time around.

But how do we learn to trust intuition? How do we become familiar with it? Besides meditation to know ourselves, what can we do daily to check into intuition?

Press pause.

I recommend pausing for a variety of reasons. Pausing gives us a moment to have our mind, body, and spirit get in sync. When I am struggling with a decision or am stressed, I pause for a moment and pay attention to what is going on inside of me. Pausing is an opportunity for the voice in my head to quiet down, and the voice in my gut to be heard.

Feel the urge, and follow it.

Our intuition can be felt physically. Whenever we feel like we fight an urge, we're fighting our truth. The urge is our intuition directing us to where we should go. When I go against my gut,

I almost always regret the decision. It rarely works out how I pictured it in my head. And even if by chance it does, I don't feel a sense of fulfilment. Intuition is a flow, and we feel in the flow of life when we follow our intuition.

Test your intuition.

When you're thinking about lunch, it's a great opportunity to stop. Stop thinking, and feel what your gut wants. Then test out your intuition. Start testing it out when driving. Just because we've always taken one road home, it doesn't mean that there isn't something new to discover by going a different road. Perhaps our gut is telling us to go that way. It might even bring on a spark of creativity!

When we test our intuition, it is an opportunity to build trust in following its directions. The more we test-drive our intuition, the more we can rely on it to bring us success in life and to bring us opportunities that we might otherwise have missed had we relied solely on our brain and its encyclopaedia of experiences.

Intuition brings true freedom and leads us away from our subconscious programming. Try it, and see what happens!

Lesson 27 | PSYCHOLOGY: The Soul is the Most Basic Unfuckwithable Essence

Worthlessness is an imagined lack of the mind's doing. Intuition is said to be the voice of the soul. Assuming this is true, then the soul is an essence that is unfuckwithable.

When we ignore our intuition, we progressively create, receive, and experience events that, well, let us know that we are being ignorant dicks. And these messages get incrementally more aggressive the longer that we ignore our intuition.

First, the feather, then, the brick, then, the truck

The masculine part of us stands so strong and stubborn in what we know that intuition is often disregarded as silly. The mind seeks and is, effectively, addicted to rational answers that it can analyse. The mind craves things that it can calculate, predict, qualify, and measure. It's performing its job perfectly by doing this. However, relying only on thought is as wise as waiting for a car to drive itself. You can pop that Tesla into autopilot, but it can only do as much as it's programmed to do. It has no innate opinion.

Your intuition doesn't give a fuck about how much you earn, how many people love you, or what your boyfriend's abs looks like. Intuition cares if you are happy and fulfilled, and it will always guide you accordingly. Unfortunately, a ton of conditioning has swayed our minds to disregard spiritual fulfilment and authenticity in place of shiny objects and short-term gratification. Alas, it creates a life of suffering and ever intensifying dissatisfaction that the consumer market banks on. Our fears and emptiness are bought and sold at our fingers tips 24/7.

Fulfilment blossoms from taking actions on what is authentically meaningful to you.

We are so fucking afraid to be still with ourselves in case we discover that we are not the lie that we have been living, the perfect avatar that can slip into society as a valued member.

Unfortunately, this inauthenticity is a shallow and empty road. Potentially, it is full of material things, but it lacks depth and love. That sucks, right? We've all most likely been here at some point or another; don't flip out too much, just start doing something about it now.

Intuition is what can guide you back to a genuine space of unconditional love, presence, and certainty from a place deep within you that is through and beyond your noggin. Your fat wallet or G cup might boost your ego enough to have you feeling superior and walking through crowds, but the feeling of superiority is a far meeker substitution for courage than true courage fuelled through authenticity, and it is sure to fade and crumble.

Have the courage, the discipline, and the intelligence to know that sitting still and cultivating this internal GPS is not only going to give you the confidence to be you but also guide you to a life of more success and fulfilment than your tiny little mind (in comparison) can comprehend.

The majority of us are trained, like soldiers, to only honour our minds. And rightly, we should. However, in this pursuit, there stands to remain a genius that we tend to swat like a meaningless fly; the genius is intuition.

CODE FIVE

FEEL IT, FREE IT

INTRO: Stay Put so You Can Be Free

The way I see it, we have two options when it comes to dealing with emotions. We can run, or we can feel. In turn, these lead to two possible outcomes. Respectively, they lead to short-term happiness coupled with deep, inner misery or temporary discomfort and a deeper, permanent state of lightness, inner peace, and joy paired with the energy to create whatever you like in your life.

Running from emotions drains us of energy. It's heavy and holds us back. It's also the perfect recipe for crafting the reincarnation of the past events that are stuck in our psyche and stimulate our emotional baggage, making it heavier and harder to let go.

Most of us have no idea that we are running away from our emotions; it's something that we are not commonly taught to consider. And do you want to know why? Because when we run from something unconsciously, we don't know that we are doing it, which means that we don't realise it's even an issue. So, we don't do anything about it. And why would we? Because running feels pretty okay, at least temporarily.

Feeling our emotions, on the other hand, requires a few practices that are rarely used effectively in our current society: vulnerability and detachment. Thus, often, feeling our emotions appears scary and unattractive. The result of practising vulner-ability and detachment—as you have already learned—requires strength and courage.

We think that we know what sets us off, but most people blame other people for how they feel. People often misun-derstand their emotions and think that what they are feeling is a result of something outside of themselves, but really, it is something that is already within, waiting to be acknowledged.

We blame our partners for pain, sadness, or a lack of love that we experience in a relationship, when really, it is all that, swim-ming within ourselves. The relationship is just a trigger, and the emotions are something that you can use as a guide. However, it is always safe to say that you must look within to find the cause. The bigger the reacting, the deeper the pain, and the more intense it is, the bigger the event from a younger age that has not yet been worked through. We may think that we are reacting to something that was said or done in the present, but we are not. We are reacting to our pain from the past.

Our triggers are there to serve us; it's epic when you think about it. Our bodies are screaming with this toxic energy, "Let me out of here," "Examine me; feel me, and let me go."

Suppressed emotions and uncomfortable feelings are the two major driving forces of our desire to stimulate, numb, and escape from the world around us.

Emotions and feelings are a very natural and beautiful response to life. Our ability to connect with others, to love, and be loved is directly linked to our ability to be vulnerable and to feel and express emotions.

Our emotions are indicators of what is going on inside of us. When we allow ourselves to feel them at the moment when they occur, as children do before they are taught that it is wrong to do so, our feelings will be very temporary. They will come and go in a natural flow. It is the suppression and repression of emotions that cause our pain to linger.

To let go and to detox from our old emotional stuff, it's vital to realise that our emotions are flag posts, guiding us back to points in our life when we had misperceptions of the wholeness of a situation. Holding onto negative emotions is like holding onto a bunch of unnecessary weight.

It's vital to work through your beliefs about emotions before attempting to feel them. These beliefs will lock or unlock your ability to experience life and let things go.

There are deeper consequences than most of us realise when we hold on to past baggage and, as a result, hold onto emotions and never truly understand how to feel them. Let me assure you that every single client out of the thousands who I have worked with on healing past trauma had to shift their perceptions and let go of what they were holding on to. They knew that they would continue to repeat the past, stay reactive, and keep self-sabotaging if they didn't. Emotions are an automatic judgment of the mind. Negative emotions like anger, resentment, guilt, greed, fear, jealousy, and insecurity are all low vibrational emotions. They're heavy in their presence of our concourses, and the longer that we hold onto these perceptions and emotions, the heavier they feel because the energy that they take from us compounds over time.

People are so afraid to feel emotions and become vulnerable to them because the weight of some emotions can feel dense and overwhelming. Their mind says, "Fuck that, let's just push that motherfucker right back to where I stored it," but it lingers, creating ever-more murkiness.

Our lack of understanding is a result of having been conditioned to bury our most uncomfortable feelings, to remain calm, and to show our happy face to the world. We have been told that it is not acceptable to express our emotions because they are seen as a sign of weakness.

Our emotions embarrass us. We fear that others will judge or reject us for displaying them, and we certainly don't want to hurt or upset anyone while doing so.

Thus, many of us have been denying our emotional pain for a very long time. We have become accustomed to unconsciously denying our emotions out of habit so that we can function in our day-to-day lives. The problem with doing this is that living is about much more than just functioning. It's the difference between existing and truly living.

We can escape, or we can feel. If all of my years of self-discovery, scrutiny, and outgrowing the pain have taught me anything, it's this; you can never run away and be truly content on the inside, not ever. The only way out is to go through.

What does feeling your emotions look like? Feeling comes in many forms, and I have learned all sorts of different tools that are included in this code. If you take away just one thing away, may it be the knowledge that you will be okay. The main reason that you want to be able to feel your emotions is that we cannot be selectively numb. If we block our pain, we block our joy. Running, resisting, and blocking emotion in any way means that we block our ability to feel anything beautiful.

We become used to this numbness. It becomes accepted, normal, and habitual. Destructive escapism goes left untreated. I've seen this in clients who come to me saying that they've been diagnosed with or suspect that they have depression. Every time this happens, we discover that it comes down to one of these things or a combination of them: lack of purpose in their life, lack of authenticity, a build-up of old emotions, or repetitive toxic thought patterns.

The ever-growing incline of antidepressants (Health at a Glance, 2015) paralleled the increasing number of people being depressed (*Major Depression Facts*). This tells us how people are numbing faster, more intensely, and more frequently, despite the evolution of our society. This all stems from what I define as internal negative validation. Imagine if the drug-free solution to many cases of depression was free and ever-available: presence and awareness.

I do not deny that antidepressants can be used to great effect. Sometimes, in my opinion, it's what people need as an in-between. If they are so low that their mind is out of balance, their body can be so detached that antidepressants can bring them some relief in the interim; drugs have a place. In that time, the person could perhaps learn to come back to themselves where there is no baggage, no pain, nothing to run from, and nothing to want or need. But that's not of commercial benefit for the people selling drugs. I'm sure if those who sold antidepressants learned how to monetise consciousness, we'd stop feeding drugs to so many depressed people. Until then, though, self-enquiry, education, and responsibility are only a choice that people can make as an alternative.

We do not lack intelligence. We simply lack the ability to understand ourselves enough to be able to help ourselves. The hell of depression is desiring to be somewhere other than where you are, or *someone* other than who you are in a life other than yours, being here but never fully accepting what is. When we do this, we abandon ourselves. A part of us dies without leaving our body. We box our soul in a cloud of darkness, of self-denial, of trapped depression by not surrendering to the life that we want and accepting responsibility for the one that we already have.

Anyone can see it, though. You don't need a certificate to understand this. You must be honest with yourself. Look around you, at the phones in the hands of the people surrounding you, at this society that bows down to the rich and famous, at the way people scramble to look like the images in the magazines, or more recently on Facebook and Instagram, and at alcohol and drug abuse. It is all right in front of us.

But the answer is to!

Connection.

Vulnerability.

Acceptance.

Awareness.

Wholesomeness.

Love.

Lesson 28

OBSERVE: When We Let Emotions Just Be, They Can Be Released

"Just like children, emotions heal when they are heard and validated."

—Jill Bolte Taylor, My Stroke of Insight

Fear of the thing itself creates more fear.

Imagine for a moment that you are not afraid of your emotions. Imagine feeling invincible, knowing that to feel is to be free and that opening yourself up would make you whole and connected to a part of yourself that recognised that you were bigger than any emotion. Imagine knowing that a feeling is a friend and you don't need to be frightened.

In this truth, you'll realise that there is no reason to abandon yourself anymore. There is no need to hold onto control. The drug of validation is empty in comparison to connecting with who you are. Be you, brave enough to face the pain and the truth, and move through it. What you need to do with that pain will become apparent when you let it be.

First, you must know that every emotion is welcome, at least for the moment that it serves its purpose, which is to show you what you have been misleading yourself about and what you've shamed, blamed, and resisted accepting. An emotion is a teacher that needs not hang around after it has been acknowledged, observed, and learned from. When you feel something, anything, try this.

Set a timer, and for 120 seconds, just sit with it. Don't judge the emotion as wrong or bad in any way. Don't try to analyse it, question it, or push it down. Do not run to your old patterns. For 120 seconds, honour it, honour yourself, and stay.

The alchemy occurs not in putting effort into change but in relinquishing control. **Do** witness what is happening with child-like curiosity, but make no meaning of it, feed it nothing more than a sense of observation. Give it love and tenderness. Greet it with acceptance. It is at that exact moment that the old, compulsive need to run and the stories behind the feelings become apparent as illusions and fall away.

When you choose to trust in yourself over your abandoning behaviour to comfort you, you will stop. When you realise—finally—that running is destroying your life on more levels than one, you will look to what is real, which is only the now. And then, you'll realise that the exhausting journey to this moment was always exactly what was going to happen because it's through our darkness that we find our light. Don't spend another second in guilt for being here. Celebrate the fuck out of it!

When your worthiness no longer takes the shape of your beliefs, you will be free to shape your life authentically with inspiration and love. When you ignore your heart's messages, you essentially render your soul homeless because you have left home. You have abandoned yourself. You ran, and you've been filling moments with doing and having instead. You form a blob in space, but you never quite allow yourself just to be.

Lesson 29 | HOME: Come Back to Yourself Through Awareness

Running or feeling your emotions: what do these comparisons look like?

- Pizza or feeling your emotions
- Wine or feeling them
- Empty sex or feeling them
- Chasing some hot guy or girl or feeling them
- Netflix or feeling them
- Exotic Peruvian plant medicine or feeling them
- Complaining about them or feeling them
- Fighting against them or feeling them

We keep our emotions cultivating dis-ease in the body while we let our painful perceptions of the past haunt us, trigger us, and leave us disempowered, broken, needing help, counselling, and probably lithium (Demartini). We store them deep in our cells until we are so built up with emotions that we explode and rip our pain, sadness, and anger at everything and everyone we encounter.

The tricky part is that avoiding the pain and, thereby, storing our emotions is so automatic. Sometimes, things impact us negatively at a time when we can't process them because of our work or family responsibilities. We momentarily feel free or fine when we do it. Running, in whatever form we choose, gives us the sensation of freedom from our pain. But what is so important to see is that when we escape, we only feel good when airborne, leaping from the frying fan to the fire.

Each time we come back down, the landing is harder, and the fire gets hotter, and the intense craving for more freedom gets dialled back up.

This is an addiction; we need more of whatever numbing agent we have chosen, and we need it more frequently.

How can you come back, when for so long, running away felt like home?

Stop.

Breathe.

Breathe again.

Close your eyes and focus on your breath.

Focus on your hands. Feel them.

Breathe again.

Awareness is the first step in excavating buried emotions. We become aware of these emotions by paying attention to our triggers. Our hot buttons, the things that make us react strongly, are indications of where to start digging. Once identified, we must allow them to surface. And once they surface, we must allow ourselves to feel them.

Looking at ourselves in ways that we are unaccustomed to is not an easy thing to do, but it is the key to emotional freedom.

What is it you're running from?

First, identify the feeling. Is it anger? What's under it? Is it insecurity? What is that insecurity from, was it three weeks ago when your boss questioned your ability? Have you been running ever since by being busy, so that 72 hours later, you still have no idea why you feel overwhelmed, and all you want is a bottle of wine and a bucket of chicken wings? So, you felt tiny and useless, what does that feeling remind you of? Is it from all of those years when your dad told you that you were a waste of space and your mum thought you were too emotional or when you were 16 and your boyfriend cheated on you?

Or is it a different emotion? Is it fear of abandonment? Are you abandoning yourself? Did your mum leave you when you were young? So now, when your friends reject you or don't call you, do you feel belittled and meaningless? Do you want to run back to the treadmill, escaping your pain through punishment or the hope for future validation of your body?

What lie is your mind luring you into? What have you believed for so long? What do you need to acknowledge to let go?

Don't be afraid to go there.

Once you find it, feel it.

Stay.

> "Staying requires being curious about who you actually are when you don't take yourself to be a collection of memories. When you don't infer your existence from replaying what happened to you, when you don't take yourself to be the girl your mother/father/brother/teacher/lover didn't see or adore. When you sense yourself directly, immediately, right now, without pre-conception, who are you?"
>
> **—Geneen Roth, Women, Food and God**

Just be present. You will not fall into a billion pieces and never be able to pick yourself up again. I promise. We don't need to fear our emotions. We fear the meaning of some of them, the perception, or the judgment.

All emotions are safe. They're messengers. Stop judging your emotions. Stop judging yourself for having emotions at all. Insecurities, fear, anger, sadness, if you fight them, they will grow; if you acknowledge them, you can get to a safe space to feel them and grow.

Let it be.

Breathe.

Say to yourself, "This is not me. This is just an emotion."

Allow enough space to distance your from it.

Accept that it's there.

And now, feel.

It might feel like you will fall apart and that it will consume you, but it won't. It's only because you've been holding on for so long that it feels like the weight behind the floodgates will surely destroy you if you open them.

And yes, perhaps you might end up in the fetal position for a few days. Crying is a release. Let it out. Be sure not to let your ego indulge in the self-fulfilment of poor me. Give yourself compassion. The bridge to realising everything that you are feeling is pure, simple awareness. We'll explore how to balance your perceptions more in Code Six when we look at nurturing your wild side.

Running fuels the fire of whatever you are running from. It takes so much courage to stay, but when you stay, you will find that your courage is endless.

Lesson 30 | VARIETY: Emotions Look and Feel Different For Us All

"Unexpressed emotions will never die. They are buried alive and will come forth later in uglier ways."

—Sigmund Freud

We all have different attitudes towards emotions. Begin with respecting your opinion about your emotions. The first clue that you're enslaved to your emotions is if you have shame, guilt, or resentment towards them.

As children, we would have witnessed and experienced the expression and reaction to emotions and began forming opinions about the wrongness and rightness of them. Some develop a resistance to emotions like anger and sadness. Some of us felt so much pain when someone projected their emotions onto us that we then suppressed our own. All emotions have their place. They all have incredible messages to give us, and for so many of us, they were shoved under the rug or deemed inappropriate.

I love the following quote by Jeffrey Eugenides in *Middlesex*, which sums up what I mean by this. He says,

"Emotions, in my experience, aren't covered by single words. I don't believe in 'sadness,' 'joy,' or 'regret.' Maybe the best proof that the language is patriarchal is that it oversimplifies feeling. I'd like to have at my disposal complicated hybrid emotions, Germanic train-car constructions like, say, 'the happiness that attends

disaster.' Or, 'the disappointment of sleeping with one's fantasy.' I'd like to show how 'intimations of mortality brought on by aging family members' connects with 'the hatred of mirrors that begins in middle age.' I'd like to have a word for 'the sadness inspired by failing restaurants' as well as for 'the excitement of getting a room with a minibar.' I've never had the right words to describe my life, and now that I've entered my story, I need them more than ever."

When we suppress emotions and feelings and do not allow them to flow freely, peace and disconnection to that emotional power are farther away because we are terrified of the pain of experiencing it. We avoid feeling vulnerable because we lack the understanding that vulnerability fosters our ability to express, create, and feel alive. When we suppress one emotion, we suppress them all. We cannot individually choose to experience positive emotions but neglect the negative ones. We will dull the sense of everything.

Like all things, emotions have energetic vibrations. We cannot see them, but we feel them. When we numb them and do not let them flow through our body of vibrating particles, they get stuck. Buried emotions will not be silenced for they are the clues to the unconscious perspective that the mind has, and they need to be acknowledged, listened to, and released to transcend the limitations of dual thinking.

Let's start with a few basic emotions and feelings.

When you read the word anger, what do you think about? What memories come to your mind when you think about anger? How do you feel within yourself when you think about anger? Think about the last time you were angry. Can you feel it? Are you scared of anger? Was anger wrong in your family?

Did anger hurt you as a child? Was it ever shown? Was it shown too much?

It is very important not to use the labelling of these emotions as a way of avoiding responsibility. For example, saying, "Oh, it was my temper," is not taking responsibility. The idea behind labelling the emotions is to help you become aware in order to take responsibility, not give it away. It would be empowering to say for example, "I felt angry and projected it," and then apologise.

There are over 6,000 words in the English language that name emotion so I cannot list them all, but here are some basic ones to start. The fundamental point that I want to install within you is that all emotions are okay. They have their place; in fact, learning or growing would be hard without them.

- Sad
- Happy
- Insecure
- Guilt
- Fear
- Trust
- Shame
- Surprise
- Joy
- Confusion
- Love
- Courage
- Overwhelm
- Embarrassment
- Peace
- Fear
- Stress
- Terror
- Excitement

- Amusement
- Hope

Exercise: Emotional Awareness

Choose three from the above list, and start to feel through them. Observe what feedback or thoughts that you get around each as you explore. Awareness is incredibly powerful. As you become aware of each reaction that you have to each emotion, remind yourself that emotions are safe and okay for you to feel.

When you feel this emotion, what do you do with it? Close your eyes, and imagine watching yourself in a previous situation when you felt angry.

Did you shrink? Did you feel guilty? Did you feel afraid of yourself? Did you suppress it? Did you make a joke to avoid it? Did you swallow it? Did you burst?

You will begin to notice your reaction to the emotion, and in those moments, you can begin to choose to react differently. That is, hopefully, to simply feel the emotion and remind yourself how safe you are.

When emotions come up, follow these six steps:

1. Notice what the emotion is, identify it. It's great to write down a few words; notice what it feels like in your body.
2. Take a breath and notice the thought that is triggering it. Is it, "I have so much to do," stimulating overwhelm or, "I am such a failure," stimulating shame, or is it something else entirely?
3. Take another breath, and focus on stilling the mind. The thought will bring about a tidal wave of emotions if you don't still it.

4. Try to find where the emotion is in your body. Pay attention to how your body feels.

5. Feel the emotion. Let it be there. Don't fight it; don't feed it with thought; don't make a story out of it. Don't judge it. Acknowledge it like a small child tugging on your shorts in need of love and compassion.

6. It will shift and change, or it will leave. If it's a layered emotion like anger, often, it will shift into something else. Repeat steps 1-6 until you get to peace, love, gratitude, or something else that is okay with you.

Sometimes, people walk around for decades holding onto anger or shame. Therefore, yoga and meditation can be a vital part of healing from old trauma as they foster a stillness that allows suppressed emotions to rise, be felt, and released.

Lesson
31 | GUILT:
Use It, and Lose It

Stop waiting for someone to fix you. Stop waiting for life to happen to you. If you wait, you'll turn around in 40 years to a life that wasn't as fulfilling as you deserved. You'll call it fate, or you'll use an even more disempowering excuse, bad luck.

Get your arse into gear, and make a difference in your life. Your life is full of the answers that you need to make changes. Stop searching outside of yourself. Stop telling yourself that it's too hard. And quit saying that it's just because you're a lazy person, an anxious person, or an insecure person; stop telling yourself lies and sabotaging your life. Stop lying to yourself that you need or prefer a more passive approach.

Bullshit. You are none of those things; those mistaken beliefs and identities do not describe you. You may have behaved that way, but that is not who you are. These descriptions are similar to the difference between screwing up and being a screw-up. We all mess up. We all act selfishly. We all get lazy. But those things do not define us. Your thoughts and words and the meaning that you make about your actions and results define your character but not your essence. So, **change them**. Change how you refer to yourself right now.

You only behaved negatively because you listened to a little voice in your head that fed your fear and fuelled your insecurities and lack of worth. You didn't know better then, but you do now.

Life doesn't wait for people who live passively and believe their untrue stories. It will keep moving, and you will miss the entire bloody point.

Only **you** can step up and live. Only **you** can take responsibility. Only **you** can make change happen.

The shit that is falling apart around you, the emotional tsunami, the car accident, the broken heart, the bout of depression, it's all feedback from life saying, "Listen the fuck up, buddy. Things have to change around here."

You need to change your actions or your perspective. That's it. You can believe the lies, or you can change. Those are our two choices as humans.

Look at your undesirable situations, and ask yourself, "How can I **be** different in this world? How can I act differently, think differently, and feel differently about the way that I am projecting and interpreting to change what I don't like?"

It is always up to you.

This responsibility does not belong to anyone else,

just you.

Lucky that you are fucking incredible, eh?

Yes, you are.

No, I am not talking to everyone,

only you.

I am talking to you, the person reading these words.

You are capable of expressing the greatness that is within you.

Start now.

Decide.

Be. Do. Have.

GREATNESS

The counsellors, the friends, the coaches, the psychologists, the healers, they're intensified reflectors of what's already inside you. They catalyse the healing process so that you can work through your issues and maximise the capacity that you have on this earth this time around. They are not the answer. They lead you to the answer, and the answer, my friend, is in you.

Let go of your self-blame. Let go of your guilt. Lose it, and move on.

Lesson 32

TRUST: The Absence of Fear

Fear and every other shadow emotion that stems from it are like armour, protecting the ego from surrendering to whatever is happening in front of us. As we have already learned, the term ego is just a term used to describe the mental image that we have of ourselves; it is a collection of thoughts perceiving, projecting, and protecting the sense of self. So, in fact, it is something that is imagined. It is in the mind, an illusion of the mind.

It's so hard to give up [insert compulsive addiction here] because engaging in your [insert compulsive addiction here] is the easiest way to leave behind your truth and cover up what is going on underneath. We run from life when life gets hard. If you can understand that, regardless of what emotion is arising, it won't be so hard. And remember to pay attention and feel the rising emotions. The desire to run is our way of putting space between where we are now and what our soul is telling us. It's a distraction by our ego to keep feeding the fear, keep us small, and stop us following our hearts, ending the need for a sense of self.

We also use emotions to rebel against something that isn't how we want it to be. Emotions are a way of standing up to the things that challenge us. Sitting too long in emotions is another form of running. Staying angry is like saying, "Universe, how fucking dare you?" When we're angry, we are trying to change who has control, but the feeling is just the pain of resistance. Anger is the heat of winding yourself up into non-acceptance.

If you learn to become okay with what is, you'll no longer feel the need to hold onto your emotions for protection.

Your armour feels safe, but it's heavy as fuck. It's too much work. Why do we put it on? Fear and lack of trust. How can we take it off?

Trust.

I can hear it already, the resistance.

"But I trusted him, and he hurt me."

"I've learned that the only person who I can trust is myself."

"If I trust these words, I may fail."

Okay, yes. Life leaves us with scars that make us bitter. Over time, our scars and bitterness make us hard and rigid. We live hard and rigid lives with hard and rigid minds. We become cold and withdrawn, and we wonder why we feel alone.

We must be flexible to be free. The beginning of living is the willingness to let what we feel is imperfect *be* imperfect, not to resolve it, twist it, or fit it into the box that we need it to fit into to feel okay. If in letting it be, we don't accept what is, and we only accept its potential to be something else that we'd prefer, we have missed the mark. We have not learned to trust. We are still looking for comfort in a reality that we perceive that we can control. We have only loved the potential that the reality could be. This is resistance.

People often think that they need a drink to calm down at the end of the day, or a joint, sex, a packet of Tim Tams, or a cig-arette. The stress is there, but with avoidance of feeling and trust, the excuses come.

"What about...?"

"What if...?"

"How can I fix this...?"

"This needs to change..."

"I'm afraid of what might happen if..."

"But..."

Trust is accepting the feeling of not needing to know; trust gives you freedom to be. Practise being okay with not knowing. It's only when we are suspended in a moment by our focused attention that we can see that we are exactly where we need to be.

If you feed your fear and live into it, you'll never land. Your potential will never truly be experienced. You'll get to the end of your days and realise that you allowed worry and fear to steal your life, that you stole your life from yourself.

When you are connected, you can still go places, but the need to know is not there. You can be free and flow. You can let life carry you where you were meant to be going in the first place before all of your resistance.

Lesson

33 | PAIN: Break the Habitual Addiction

Why do we hold onto pain when it hurts us?

We turn to the belief that we are our emotions because it gives our sense of self a dark, yet gripping and addictive strength. It is an internal validation.

The reason that so many people find it hard to let go of their problems is because it means that they'd have to let go of the easiest and most subtle form of bringing importance and attention to themselves, which is the internal validation and attachment that they have to the stories and the external validation and attachment that they receive from others.

Most people would slap me if I said this to their face because, of course, no one wants to hear that their problems are a self-fulfilling prophecy that only they can change, especially if they've spent a whole lifetime feeling like the outer world was against them.

Often, we don't just have one emotional wave; we have multiple because of the mind's automatic resistance to everything, including emotions themselves. We have the emotion. Then, we have the guilt and judgment of having the emotion. All of us feel this guilt and judgment unless we allow ourselves to be present and hear the call of our soul, which is trying to tell us that these stories that we are telling ourselves are not true.

We are nearly drowning in emotion, feeling like there is no way out. But you need to know, that while you may feel things,

- You are not your emotions.
- You are not depressed.
- You are not anxious.
- You are not anger.
- You are not shame.
- You are not worthlessness.
- You are not guilty.
- You are not stress.
- You are not even happiness.

You have thoughts, but you are not what you think.

You are not a failure or a fuck-up even if you have failed and fucked up.

You are not broken.

You are love.

Lesson 34

SUFFERING: Focus Your Attention Elsewhere

Suffering is the consistent build-up of negative emotions fuelled by focusing on what we don't have.

We choose to focus on what we *think* that we need to create a positive emotion, but an emotion is only the physical expression of our thoughts.

Take the fear of missing out, for example. We are spoiled to have so many options. There used to be three fucking ice cream flavours: strawberry, chocolate and vanilla. It was straightforward. Now, there are 7 billion choices. We have anxiety and stress about making decisions. We are paralysed by the fear of missing out on all of the flavours.

This example is similar to the everyday stress that we experience. We ask, "What should I do with my life?" "Who should I be?" "Am I doing this happy/purpose/relationship/career thing right?" "What if I do it wrong?" and demand, "Someone, give me the answers!"

The fear of missing out (FOMO) is a great cause of both anxiety and sabotage. The excuse, "I love variety," has rung through my ears countless time from clients who want help becoming more disciplined. FOMO is just another story distracting us from truly sinking into life and enjoying it fully.

It is the chase of fleeting pleasure instead of exercising responsibility and strength to sit in and fully surrender to life.

Those classified in the millennial group, those born after 1984, are introduced into a world that has over exposed them (us, I am also in this group) to such enormous amounts of opportunity. This opportunity, while incredible, also serves as an immense stimulation and overwhelm to us and has snowballed now more than ever.

The anxiety of not doing enough quickly enough and doing it better than anyone else is ever growing. Millennials struggle to master the art of patience and discipline as much as previous generations. Our world now buys and sells time through products that constantly make life easier, and thus, we find it even harder to switch off and recognise the exact cause of our anxiety, fear, stress, and depression is the opportunity, choice, and convenience that we are constantly seeking.

We only seek advice when we don't want to face the truth that we already know. We confuse ourselves, so we don't have to make a choice and take responsibility for any consequences (unconsciously). We ask for help. Not deciding is a decision though, and it destroys us. We blame the outside word for our paralysis and procrastination.

What might your life look like if you chose to take responsibility, even if it stings? Say you created a situation that you now have a problem with. You can change it. Even if it feels like you have no power, by taking responsibility and letting go of blame, you retrieve that power back.

It is up to you.

Forget the excuses.

You've got this.

Stop focusing on all the other flavours or what you *think* you need to be happy. Drop this fantasy of, "When I [insert something **more** to do], then I will be fulfilled/enough/happy/satisfied/beautiful." This will only create more feelings of not being fulfilled/enough/happy/satisfied/beautiful. Decide to choose to be happy, and create your own damn ice cream. Forget the rest.

Lesson

35 | LISTEN: Pay Attention, and Let Go

"I believe in intuitions and inspirations... I sometimes ***feel*** *that I am right. I do not* ***know*** *that I am."*

—Albert Einstein

Intuition is deciding without our brain necessarily being able to understand why. It is unbiased by fear and doesn't bother battling with the incomparable consequences of social non-conformity. It guides you to do what you need to do without fuss; it is only fear and logic that make the fuss.

You can combine logic with intuition, but if you ignore intuition, you will know about it. How? The suffering in your life will increase. When your life keeps giving you the results that you do not want, you can guarantee that you have ignored your intuition. You didn't listen. You have run away for so long that you are desensitised.

Intuition requires the consistent practice of connection. And it is strengthened and clearer each time that you listen to it. Its subtlety and light can be snuffed out with a huff of doubt and uncertainty.

Through science, we can prove theories, but through intuition, we discover and create. Thinking energy is heavy and sticky. It is thick and weighted. Hence, it receives our attention first. Intuitive sensory information, on the other hand, can be lighter in nature. It can be more nuanced and sensitive, and often, we need to be quieter and stiller to hear it.

It is as if thinking information is the extrovert in your mind, and the intuitive sensory information is the introvert. Neither is right or wrong; we need both.

Every one of us is gifted with intuition. When we rise to the challenge of remaining connected and breaking free from the addiction of our thoughts, we can feel it.

I started using the following method to help my clients move the confusion of the mind to feel what they intuitively knew was right.

First, focus entirely on your belly for 60 seconds. Whenever the mind drifts, bring it back without judgment or effort. Focus on the belly moving and count your breaths, one for in, two for out, three for in, four for out. Once you get to ten, start counting backwards.

Next, focus entirely on the sensations in your body and continue the effortless breathing up to ten again. When you ask yourself a question that you're trying to make a decision about, what does it feel like? Where is there tension? Where do you feel it?

Your body will communicate to you what you need to know. There is no running, only connection. You already knew the answer but were scared to admit the answer because of one fear or another.

This breathing and noticing sensations in the body is a form of a meditation. Meditation is connection. This practice shakes up your connection with your intuition, your inner knowingness that ducks under the mind.

And training ourselves to duck under our thoughts is why we must get connected in the first place.

For a reminder of how you can do that and why else you would want to, flick back to the beginning of this code. Or stick around for Code Six; we'll be nurturing your wild side!

NURTURE YOUR WILD SIDE

INTRO: Go Wild

Most people live a sheltered, uninspired, or uninspiring life because they never realise who they are and their full potential. Fuck that.

I know it's scary as hell to follow your wild heart. I can hear all the buts already. *"But Amber, it's all well and good to say run wild and free, but the reality is that I have three kids, I'm a single mum, and I have a mortgage."*

Shut up, ego. Yeah, that's right. Have you any idea how easy (yet devastating) it is just to say, "Well, I can't because…"? It's easy to find excuses; excuses are where fear hides. We use time, money, relationships, and our career as reasons to hold ourselves back. I could sit here all day and quote stories about the thousands of miraculous people who were not willing to settle for their bullshit and who beat the odds no matter what, but then, the book would never end.

Okay, I'll just give you a few.

The first story is the story of my dad. After more than two decades of battling an incurable disease and nearly dying just before my 23rd birthday, he still was wanting to sell his business as a boilermaker after a very, very long time. I know when I say this, he will laugh and agree, but my Dad loves a good excuse, "Yeah, but it's just hard, darling. You know?" It was a hard slog for a long time. First, he didn't die. We don't really know how. I asked him once, and he said that after I had come to see him into his 14-hour surgery, he decided that he wanted to live. The doctors were so surprised that he made it through the surgery, and they are surprised that he is still alive. My step Mum, I am certain, has a lot to do with keeping him alive; she is a woman of true bravery. It takes more strength than I think most of us can ever imagine, looking after someone who spent two decades in and out of the hospital. Thanks, Shazz, I love you!

Moving forward, he was a man with barely any life in him. He had no money in the bank, and after years of just scraping through, he and my step mum sold the welding business and bought a music shop. Now, for context, I grew up with my Dad while he was in his mid-twenties. He would strum to ZZ Top and Jimmy Hendrix on his Fender guitar in between plaiting my hair and packing my lunches for school. I have a photo of me at two years old in a rock magazine, looking up at him on stage as he jammed out in a band. Music was his life force. Despite having no money and very little self-belief and hope, at the age of 50 after never having made it in the views of society, he followed his fucking bliss. He is my everyday hero.

And now, a classic hero, a story from Akanksha Prabhune, published on Storypick.

"This woman needs no introduction. Her books have sold more than 400 million copies worldwide. But there was a time in her life when she was diagnosed with clinical depression and contemplated suicide. Her marriage had failed, and she was jobless with a dependent child. She signed up for government aid (she was so poor, she could not afford to support herself and her daughter), describing her economic status as being 'poor as it is possible to be in modern Britain, without being homeless.'

"In 1990, while she was on a four-hour-delayed train trip from Manchester to London, the idea for a story of a young boy attending a school of wizardry 'came fully formed' into her mind. In 1995, she finished the manuscript of her first book on an old manual typewriter. The book was submitted to twelve publishing houses, all of which rejected the manuscript. Editor Barry Cunningham from Bloomsbury advised her to get a day job since she had little chance of making money from writing children's books.

"Today, she is United Kingdom's best-selling living author, with an estimated fortune of **£560 million**, ranking her as the twelfth richest woman in the UK. She is none other than J.K Rowling – the creator of the Harry Potter series. Saying that the Harry Potter franchise was and is a success would be an understatement."

And a hero, who probably no one knows about, who I thought rocked at life, again from Akanksha.

"A prodigy rock climber, by age eight he had scaled the face of the 11,627-foot Mount Temple in the Canadian Rockies, and by 17 he was acknowledged to be one of the best climbers in the United States. In January 1982, after having ascended a difficult technical ice route in Huntington Ravine on Mount Washington in New Hampshire, Herr and a fellow climber Jeff Batzer were caught in a blizzard and became disoriented, ultimately descending into the Great Gulf where they passed three nights in –29 °C degree temperatures. By the time they were rescued, the climbers had suffered severe frostbite. Both of Herr's legs had to be amputated below the knees; his companion lost his lower left leg, the toes on his right foot, and the fingers on his right hand. While a postdoctoral fellow at MIT in biomedical devices, he began working on advanced leg prostheses and orthoses, devices that emulate the functionality of the human leg. Using specialized prostheses that he designed, he created prosthetic feet with high toe stiffness that made it possible to stand on small rock edges the width of a coin, and titanium-spiked feet that assisted him in ascending steep ice walls. He used these prostheses to alter his height to avoid awkward body positions and to grab the hand and foot holds previously out of reach. His height could range from five to eight feet.

"As a result of using the prostheses, Herr climbed at a more advanced level than he had before the accident, making him the first person with a major amputation to perform in a sport on par with elite-level, able-bodied persons."

I have said it before, and I will say it again; be your own fucking hero.

Just know this; if it's a limit; it's a story

(Aside from the laws of the universe around physics, but even then, some people are proving those laws breakable.)

The major role of all three careers that I have had—being a personal trainer, a coach, and working in the hospital—was listening to people justifying why they were holding themselves back. And I have concluded that we are all dickheads. We believe our bullshit so easily. It's a waste.

Maybe, it's time you asked some different questions.

This is what usually happens when I make that suggestion. You stick to your same self-preserving behaviour, but you convince yourself that you *are* living. Then, you watch an inspiring YouTube video, go to a seminar, or get your heart broken, and you realise that you were never really living in the first place. You are sleeping. Sleeping is easily identified by the measurement of the excuses endlessly streaming from your mouth and the fears building on top of each other in your mind.

And that's it. You roll with that and call it fate. You drink down coffee and jam doughnuts. You cover your self-esteem issues with a drink each night. Sadly, it's a normal illness that the world is sick with, but that does not make it okay. You continue, day after day, off to work to pay the bills. You might even have a family and love your babies, but you've still got this blank space inside of you that you've ignored.

And then, one day, you stop and ask yourself in the middle of sex with your partner who you know doesn't really love you, in a home that you won't pay off before you die, craving the holiday that you've been talking about for years, *Isn't there more than this?*

Suddenly, the woman who you follow on social media no longer sounds narcissistic like she once did. She speaks to your soul. And you decide enough is enough. It's time to break free. It's time to value your life.

Dear fucking gosh,

choosing to be free and nurturing your wild side is hard fucking work.

There is no magic pill.

#werk

Being unfuckwithable takes work.

I have said this many times; it's the tiny things that add up. It is the discipline to wake up and not pick your phone up and scroll through your emails. It is walking through nature, not to be anywhere, not to lose weight, not to escape, but to simply enjoy it. It is to be able to take a compliment. It is to be able to give a compliment. It is only saying yes to the things that are an absolutely fucking yes. It is finding your voice and using it.

Everything counts. This code is the work of being unfuckwithable.

The fuck yeses, my friend, are your wild side, and we are about to nurture it.

Lesson

36 | INTEGRITY: Stop Running, and Live with Integrity

Live with fucking integrity, not just integrity,
fucking integrity,
which means that you do what you say and say what you mean,
always.

Make every word count.
Don't be afraid to say no or to be wrong or challenged.
Stand your fucking ground.
Don't waste your words talking about others.
Fuck that. It takes energy.

Make every thought a thought about what you want not about
what you don't want.

Stop making excuses. Stop it.
Stop believing in fear.

Stop running.

We run.
Oh, dear, do we run.

We run to places,
people,
things,
and we look for someone who will validate our fears.

We look because we are afraid. We are terrified. We think we're
running from something genuine, but that's how wrong we

are. It's our fear's fear of finally realising that there is nothing at all to the fear except the light that shines from within. Fear is the story that keeps us from understanding how fucking brilliant that we all. Fear keeps us on a spinning wheel of thought, anxiety, and stress.

We run to try to free ourselves from fear only to find more of it on a road that never ends.
We seek comfort, something to relieve us from the anxiety of the noise in our mind that sends ripples of discomfort through our body.
We run to find shelter from our emotions, to find love, and other drugs.
We try to make ourselves safe by covering our discomfort with what feels good.
We run to escape.

When there is something amiss, our mind tells us that what we need is someplace beyond ourselves.
Stop.
Come home, right now.
Breathe.

In yoga, there is a saying, "Let the sweat scratch your itch."
Instead of wiping the sweat rolling over every inch of our bodies, we let the natural consequence sort out the irritation.
Do this with fear.
Do this with impulse.
Do this with thought.

Let them scratch themselves. When you don't give into its bullshit, when you stop paying it attention and let it be instead of wishing it will leave, you'll notice in minutes that it will fade.

Do not allow your mind to convince you that running will leave what you fear behind. It will only strengthen your fear. Do not

allow it to show you images of a life without fear when you run
as if keeping on running will take you to where you want to go.

The only place to go is home, with you, in you, always.
Be there.

Believe in yourself, even if you don't know how.
Give it a go.
Ask yourself, "What if I did know how?"
For fuck sake, give up the pity parties.
Compassion is powerful, yes, *but do not wallow.*

Take time to feel; it's freeing.
Take time to rest; it's rejuvenating.
Take time to be still; it's living.

Do not take the time to indulge in pity.

Do things that align with your soul, for goodness sake; have
intention in everything that you do,
Every step that you take,
Every meal that you eat,
Every joint that you smoke,
Every tear that you shed,
Every yoga that class you attend,
Every job that you do,
Every person who you fuck.

Do everything with the intention of creating a life that is yours.
This will all probably rock your world.
A lot of stopping doing will be required from you.
So, just do one at a time.

Fear is a shadow of your light.
You cannot light a candle without casting a shadow.
Everything has an equal and opposite reaction.

Your light and your truest path will be met with equal amounts
of fear and challenge.
That's how you know what to do and where to go.
Let fear lead you.

Laugh at fear.
It will dissolve and show its shadow, so all that is left is light.

Live with fucking integrity.

Lesson
37 | LOCATION:
Where the Ego Lives

I've got to give it credit; the ego is a scheming thing. It hides behind almost everything.

Clients always ask me, "Is this my ego? Is that my ego?"

So, I came up with this simple, little ego test as an activity that you can use day-to-day to exercise your unfuckwithableness.

Exercise: Finding your Ego

When a thought arises, examine it.

Does the content of the thought suggest a sense of superiority or inferiority towards yourself or another in any way?

Does the thought believe that it's good or bad, better or worse, right or wrong?

- Is there judgment behind it or a need to defend?
- It can be so subtle. Consider these:
- Is there any puffing up or shrinking whatsoever?
- Is there any criticism of self or another?
- Is there any need to feel better than?
- Is there any story about being less than?
- Is there any hint of having problems?
- Is it subconsciously creating problems?
- Is it sabotaging?
- Is it complaining? *Ahhh, complaining makes us so important!*

- Is it criticising yourself or another?
- Is it trying to justify itself?

What comes from your mouth? If the ego benefits, it will find a way to sneak in. That, my friend, is what the ego sounds like.

That's right, that, "Holy fuck, I get it," feeling that you just had is what the gurus call awakening. You realised that almost every single thought and conversation that you have stems from the ego. Yes, you just realised that almost every single thought is filtered through judgement.

Below are nine signs that show that our ego is in control.

- The need to be right
  - *The ego wants to be right, better than, and perfect.*
- The inability to see faults or get feedback even if it's true and valid.
- Growth can't happen when we are so busy defending our rightness that we can't hear feedback or different points of view.
  - *The lack of patience*
    The ego is in a constant rush. And though the universe tells us to slow down in many mysterious ways, we remain impatient in our endeavours. Inside each of us lies the voice of reason. Despite the voice being quite loud, we deliberately choose to ignore it and go ahead with what the ego is whispering.
- Drama
  - *The more drama that we create, the more distractions that we have to keep us from our truth.*
- Scapegoating
  - *This happens when we blame or hold a grudge against something or someone, including other races, religions, gender, vocations, entities or individuals, especially events and situations.*

- Thinking that your search for spiritual enlightenment makes you omniscient
    - *It just makes you a dick that grasps onto a new sense of self, uses different words, wears different clothes, and uses words like enlightenment, ayahuasca and consciousness over lunch.*
- The need to be the best
    - *This problem has serious effects on mankind; it's fucked up a lot of authentic goals. It has driven people away from their real goals and their real dreams.*
- Playing the blame game
    - *Imagine a world in which people admit when they went wrong. How beautiful would that world be? Imagine the conversations if people were honest. "Bill, did you cheat on Hillary or not?" "Yeah, yeah, I did." Okay."*
- Believing that we are not good enough
    - *The ego would not emphasise the benign traits. Again, it needs a story to tell. And to tell that story, it needs proof to support its statement. Thinking that we are not good enough is an excuse that our ego creates to stop us from thriving in our life. It prevents us from going forwards; its main aim is to keep us where we are.*

So, what do you do about it? Be okay with it. Seriously, there is no right or wrong.

When you hear you are doing this wrong, you can just come back to simplicity:

It's okay to feel what you are feeling.

It's okay not to be perfect.

It's okay not to understand.

It's okay to be confused.

It's okay to fail.

It's okay to change your mind.

It's okay not to follow through.

It's okay to be human.

Lesson

38 | FEAR: It's Okay to be Scared

I want you to know that it is okay to be scared. In fact, most people fear their greatness, so you are not alone. They are so scared that they will constantly return to the sweet addiction of their old, toxic, ego-led belief systems day after day and they will return to the baggage and put the masks in place to hide from their light. Don't be afraid, but be okay with the fact that you will be afraid.

Let it go. To let go, you must feel. And it might seem scary as heck at first because we have lost our sense of feeling in today's world. But I promise that it will be the most liberating thing that you can ever do. Once you tap into that space, your life will be limitless. Until then, your ego and fear-based justifications will run and hide from emotions that you feel at your core because they feel unstable, untrustworthy, and painful.

Open your big heart. You are worthy of love. You do not need anyone's approval. Stop competing with the world. Stop competing with yourself. You are not your body. You are not your achievements. You are not others' opinions. You are not the attention that you get from that boy or girl. You are not the fear that people have of you.

You are a shining, energetic being of fucking epic love.

Let it shine, and don't ever shy away from the magnitude of your life, especially the freedom part; it's that bit that scares people the most. Free from form, free from the external stuff, free from the body, the success, the fame, the trophies of life, and the gratification, you are enough, and you don't need all those things to prove it.

You are equal to all of your greatest heroes and enemies at the same time. Letting go means being free, free from a sense of me and importance, free from blame and judgment.

There is no need to run away from your light. The light that you feel shining in when you show up to the world, both perfect and broken all at once, is not a light of judgment. It is your light and greatness reflecting at you. Do not fear it.

You are loved, right now, without the masks.

I see you.

We all see you.

But you must see yourself to be free.

You might fear that freedom.

You will fear it if you believe that all of those things are who you are.

Let it go.

Let love live.

Let life thrive.

Lesson 39 | YOGA: How Yoga Makes Us Unfuckwithable

I cannot stress this lesson enough; yoga is a game changer, at least it was for me.

What is it in your life that you can say the same thing about?

If you can take my experience with Bikram yoga and find a similar condition through a sport, hobby, or career, then do it. It will be one of the most transformational accelerants to becoming unfuckwithable that you could ever do.

To brief you quickly on Bikram yoga, depending on the seriousness of the teacher—some are much stricter than others—here is a standard environment in a Bikram yoga class.

There is a small 1m x 1m podium at the front, with wall to wall mirrors across the wall that you face and, generally, another mirror in the room, taking up a full wall as well.

There are lines across the room on which you align your yoga mat halfway across; they are used for alignment during the class.

The temperature is set at 37-40 degrees Celsius. The humidity is brought up around 40-55%.

Yogis stand on the mat for 90 minutes while the teacher speaks a dialogue, and again depending on their strictness, sometimes verbatim, from a script that they learn at a Bikram yoga teacher training. Most teachers have a variation of this, but essentially, the core of it is the same. There are 26 postures in the Bikram series, each of which is done twice except the last posture.

It's hot, really fucking hot. And you breathe through your nose, which activates your parasympathetic nervous system, placing your body into a meditative state of rest and digest, activating the production of progesterone, lowing cortisol, balancing hormones, digesting your food, etc. All breathing is done this way except for the first and last breathing exercises, which you exhale through your mouth. The class is done with the instruction to connect with your reflection in the mirror. There is no talking except the teacher, and the delivery is not unlike a drill sergeant for the hardcore teachers. Of course, again, it varies; I've met a few softer-spoken Bikram teachers. The class is an epic, physical detox, mental discipline training, and spiritual evolutionary session.

The teachers, as I mentioned earlier, often say, "Let the sweat scratch your itch." If you are seen constantly adjusting your mat, clothes, hair, wiping away sweat, the teacher will pull you up or give a general instruction to the class, to still yourself and avoid any impulse to adjust and move. There is also only one official water break, about 20 minutes in after the warm-up when the class is instructed only ever to sit out or move between postures. This reminder is said during the break to keep the presence during the class strong and not distract other participants.

Because of this disciplined nature, Bikram Yoga teaches the greatest philosophies of self-mastery and life mastery that one could ever reach for outside a hot room in just 90 minutes. Now, you can simply find a practice in life that reflects the following principles If Bikram isn't available to you or if you feel like it isn't your thing. In general, all forms of yoga hold these philosophies; I found Bikram Yoga to be the most beneficial for me.

YOGA: Embracing An Unfuckwithable Life on The Mat

It broke down codependence on others. Although it is an incredible community, we are solo on that mat, which means it is just you and your battle with fear to face alone. We are forced to face our demons without running.

It taught me to let go of control, and it taught me impermanence; one of the fundamental principles is to be able to surrender and accept life in its wholesomeness, exercise vulnerability, and access authenticity. In yoga, you learn very quickly that the more you fight against yourself, the harder it is.

I learned to submit myself to suffering. A great mentor and yoga teacher of mine, Aaron Tselepy, always spoke about the necessity of submitting ourselves to suffering. When we can master stillness in an atmosphere of great physical, mental, emotional, and spiritual pressure, it enhances each moment of life, making it more exceptional and more expansive than ever before.

It humbled me. Every single class is different. The thing about yoga is it brings us back to our bodies. It forces us to see what we are often too busy to notice or do not want to admit. Some days, my practice is on point; I'm focused, strong, and steady. Other days, I'm tight, tired, sore, and irritated. Yoga picks up the uncomfortable pieces of ourselves and shows us them. We can practice bringing compassion and change into our life to adjust what has been out of place. From not enough sleep or water, to overworking, eating too much sugar or not dealing with the suppressed anger, Bikram Yoga will show you, and it will force you to face it and own it.

It helped me let go of not feeling good enough. An extension of number four, there was no one to validate me in class. There is very little approval or well done in most yoga classes. Unlike social media, yoga is not filled with affirmation outside of yourself. In yoga, you must be your own hero, supporter, and lover. After about 12 months I remember walking into class, seeing the reflection of my body in the mirror, and instead of the usual, automated criticism of me being too muscly or not lean enough that my ego threw at me, I heard and *felt*, "Wow, I am so beautiful and strong."

I felt so much love. This is the practice of loving yourself from the inside out, the connection, presence, and authenticity that is possible when we learn to still our mind and see what's there, instead of only seeing what our minds filter the world as. We are forced to feel. If you do not connect with your body, you'll injure yourself; it is as simple as that. Every day is different. If you go in trying to get the same result, same depth, and same length of holding a posture, you will learn that this pursuit ends terribly.

It forced me to feel emotions. In the book *The Divided Mind*, Dr. John Sarno explains, "The purpose of the pain is to divert attention from what's going on emotionally and to keep you focused on the body." (*The Divided Mind* is a book by a surgeon who discusses the major role of our mind in creating physical symptoms. It was the first book that I purchased after I left the hospital, and it gave me the permission to break free and walk away from Western medicine without too much hesitation.)

Energetically, we feel emotions in our body daily. Yoga helps shift the emotions that don't sit well with us through us. Some postures do this more than others. There have been times when I have wept through an entire class. I didn't know why this happened many times; I only knew that something needed to come up, and yoga was that catalyst for me; it gave me the space to let it move through.

It got me out of my head. Bikram is often called "the 90 minutes of open eye meditation" because you are constantly looking at your reflection in a mirror, focused on yourself and your breath. You are under so much physical discomfort that if you stop breathing or don't control the pace and depth of your breath, you might pass out or feel sick. And let me tell you, if your mind drifts to a negative thought in the middle of a single leg balancing posture, you WILL wobble and most likely fall. In yoga, when you're in your head, you're dead.

It taught me patience and self-control physically and mentally. Apart from the very apparent shift in energy, the extreme depth, and transformational benefits, which make one unfuck-withable, the act of yoga and connection (meditation) are not instant. We must practice patience and discipline. Yoga stops us from giving into impulsive needs and allows us to be comfortable with discomfort. Yoga and meditation are like condoms; they don't always seem useful, but when we need them, they save our arses.

It taught me to go with the flow. It taught me that life, postures, teachers, temperatures, our bodies, and mental states are always different, but we must accept them anyway.

Lesson
40 | REJECTION: Stop Wasting Your Potential Because You Fear Rejection

All too often, someone with fuck loads of potential looks me in the eye and tells me that they don't feel worthy.

Well, guess what, this is a message to every person who has ever felt that way; there is a depth within you untapped and untamed. It's ancient, and it's unfuckwithable. Those words seem so distant for many, but they're not. Those words are far from distant. In fact, those words already inside of you.

You are a soul, and that soul is a force to be reckoned with. It marches to the beat of its own drum. No one can say to your soul, "You don't measure up," or, "Your boobs are a funny shape," or, "Your Target workout gear isn't as cool as Lulu Lemon, and it's shit," or, "You can't do that for yourself; don't be so selfish."

Your soul laughs that bullshit off. It's bulletproof.

Your breath is an anchor. Use it to blow away the thoughts and protect yourself from being sucked into the emotional tornados of insecurity and anxiety. Breathe. Feel yourself, your true self. It glimmers inside, and it feels fucking radical. That's you. You are not the voice. You are not the negative bullshit stories.

The stories only seem real because they've been playing on repeat for so long, so you live according to them. But now, you have proof that you need to reject the stories. The only way out is to make a choice.

Choose to march to the sound of your soul. Choose to let go of doubt, bullshit excuses, and "I cant's."

I know that you have felt that shit, but you are ready. I know it's scary, but that's normal. You must trust that when you let go of who you think that you are, who you really are will show up, and you will finally be free.

The voice, it will still be there, but once you get a glimpse of your soul, once you reach up and take down the mask for a second, as vulnerable and scary and uncomfortable as that may seem, you can never turn back.

Come one, gorgeous soul, shine. It's calling you; can you hear it?

To be honest, it's illogical. That's called intuition. Follow it. You are shifting at a deep level. Surrender. Let it in. Let down the guard. Open up, and come on out.

See you on the other side, my love.

Lesson

41 | EVERYTHING: You Cannot Have it All

Greed
Want
More
Pining
Jealousy
Overdrive

We all know by now that the voice in our head is not an honest voice with a true perspective. Fear is always telling us that what we have and who we are is not enough.

We seem to think that we can have it all. The perfect life, 100% awesome, 100% of the time.

Life is a journey of growth and decay. Having it all is realising and owning this truth, in every aspect of yourself and life.

This might look like surrendering to a week where things just feel tough or a dip in profit or very low physical strength. It might mean seeing that relationships ebb and flow and that the crop isn't always yielding exactly what we want from it.

This may sound a little opposing to all of the other parts of the book that point to our limitlessness, but the truth is, we must remember that there will always challenges and an ultimate balance in life. Your *all* is defined by your ability to find meaning and magic in life, and in that sense, you can have it all.

To see that dark times, precede light and vice versa.

Don't fear the darker aspects, they are a trigger for change, preparation for growth and ever so continuously teaching you to master the art of not giving to many fucks in life.

Let go, let it flow happen to you and for you.

Having it all is not about being the best, making the most money, feeling 'in love' all the time, making gains at the gym every week or getting a promotion each quarter.

Having it all in this aspect is what takes us into dark places of shame and guilt.

Choose to see all, as yin and yang and then all become right now, every single moment.

That's your choice; that's you being in charge.

Lesson 42 | HEROES: Be Your Own Fucking Hero

Everyone loves a good hero's journey. It's written in our neurology, in our collective consciousness.

Stop waiting for someone else to save you.

Mostly, what happens is that they try to help, and we don't want to be helped. Yeah, that's right. We love our problem too much. The help that we get doesn't come in the right way, not because we need something different, but because we are attached to our problem, and the ego will argue with any solution. There isn't a right way because, if we're honest, we don't want the problem to go away. We'd have to find a solution and that would mean giving up our pity party.

(*Note: I think there is value in healthy forms of empathy and validation, but in this state, usually, empathy can perpetuate the victim mentality.*)

Eventually, after no one rescues us, this forces us to realise that we are the only ones who can be there for ourselves.

It's not an "I'm alone" mindset. It's about realising the opposite. You are always fully supported by yourself when you choose to be. Don't resent the ones who you love because they cannot be there when you feel like you need them to be. Start being there for yourself. Be the strength that you are looking for inside another. Take the opportunity to dig deep inside yourself, and choose you. Let go of resentment, and find a way to joyfully choose yourself.

Everyone wants to be saved because everyone loves the story of the hero. But you must be your own hero. You need to be your own mentor, every single day and have the courage to catch your mind when it creates falsified stories of self-wrongness and self-righteousness.

Lesson 43 | OVERFLOW: Fill Yourself from the Inside Out

If you want more of anything in your life, stop searching outside of yourself for it. I was reminded of this when I was struggling for inspiration for this book and on the hunt for it constantly. I had convinced myself that I needed inspiration to write. And therefore, I become an inspiration addict. I couldn't write without opening up another book, watching a YouTube video, doing yoga, or scanning Pinterest.

I lost my power by believing that I didn't already have it inside. I believed that I was missing a piece of the puzzle, and I needed something external to make me whole.

This works the same with everything in life.

Love

Money

Friendships

Food

Experiences

Knowledge

Acceptance

The more that we seek these things outside of ourselves, the emptier that we will feel and the more reliant we are on the next hit to fill us up.

When you turn to others, to money, success, drugs, clothes, yoga (yes, yoga can be abused) and approval to fill yourself up, a part of your soul dies. It cries as it watches you continue in the rat-race of life. This pattern of life deepens your emptiness and fuels your insecurities with intermittent moments of relief in each hit of your chosen drug.

External gratification is an addictive poison worse than Heroin when *relied on* for happiness.

Our need for more fuels our emptiness inside. You must give it up to experience your fullness and truly be fulfilled. You must listen to your heart, follow your intuition and ignore logic when logic tells you that your soul is wrong. Look at what you have inside. Feel it for fuck sake. Stop suppressing your intuition. You are an endless garden of the seeds that you plant and feed in your mind. Which seeds are you sowing, fear or love?

You must choose.

You are already endless inspiration and acceptance. You are enough. All the rest is bubble and squeak. You have everything you need. It's there. Lift up your fears with breath, and you won't just see it, you will feel.

And then suddenly, the Facebook scrolling, the unnecessary food, the empty sex, and the dependence on booze to relax you will feel empty, and you will be full.

CHOOSE LOVE

INTRO: Unconditional Love

By now you have probably realised that when I talk about love, I am talking in terms of our level of connection and the action potential that our connection creates in our life.

Let's bring back in my nerd flick fetish.

In Star Wars, Obi-Wan Kenobi introduced Skywalker and most of us, to the force with this statement: 'It's an energy field created by all living things. It surrounds us and penetrates us; it binds the galaxy together.'

Love, energy, soul......I feel these cross over each other and that the 'force' is essentially, 'the force life'. This force can yield epic things in life. We can wield it when we are grounded, become still and connect with ourselves. We can all be our own Jedi masters, you know, the good kind.

We must disconnect from our mental matrix and connect with life and most of all, take responsibility for it.

"Do or do not. There is no try."

—Yoda

The more we practice being in the space of connection, the less friction we experience within our emotions.

The less our mind is running the show, the more heart, soul, and oomph that you have behind what you do and the less bullshit that you will accept because you exercise authentic boundaries.

You will become more badass through a space of integrity, empowerment, and transformation that ripples through your energy and decisions.

You can be living on purpose and yet allow a thought to creep in and let it simmer in your mind and body, like, "What's everyone else doing? Am I doing enough right now?" You might find that you'll have the urge to obsessively scroll through Instagram for three hours. You must make a choice,

A choice to say no the excuses
A choice to say yes to owning your power
A choice not to blame, but take responsibility
A choice not to project, but go within, observe, and let go
A choice not to shrink and listen to fear, but to walk beside it, letting fear be your guide to evolution and growth rather than a driving energy
A choice to feel emotions rather than numb them
A choice to constantly practice observing your mind with a sense of humour and enlightenment instead of forgetting it and all of the beliefs about the world and yourself are not who you are
A choice to direct your perspective to see the wholeness
A choice to embrace your imperfect humanness
A choice to express your unique values and purpose as a soul
A choice to only live an absolutely fucking yes life

Lesson
44 | OPPOSITES:
Love Has No Opposite

Love doesn't have an opposite. Love is a choice, a choice to let go of all the resistance to what you cannot control or change.

You cannot enjoy love if you do not believe that you are worthy of it. It is not discrete in its selection of who is deserving.

Love does not have an opinion. Like the sun, love doesn't look at certain people and say, "Nope, soz, you don't earn enough." The sun doesn't say, "Hey, you know, you're not perfect, so I won't be shining my light on you." The sun doesn't give a shit about what colour your skin is, what size pants you wear, what your savings account looks like, or the title next to your name.

It shines regardless of what you have done or not done in your life. It will give you its power and energy regardless of whether you believe you deserve it. Love is the same. When you don't love yourself, you aren't open to receive the love that is always ready and waiting.

Whether you feel love or not must not depend on whether you are being given it. It is always there. The intensity of how you feel it changes based on how open you are to it, how accepting you are of yourself, and how accepting you are of love.

Love is not exclusive to those who love themselves. It just cannot be felt fully by those who don't. So, how to love yourself? Stop thinking. Stop letting the noise of your ego keep you away from experiencing what you were born to experience.

I believe in love a little different than the standard. I believe that love is seeing life as it is rather than as you think it should be. When we are in a state fear, there is no room for love. And when we are in a state of love, there is no room for fear.

It's a choice.

Love doesn't have an agenda. Love is being grateful instead of expectant. When you choose love, you are coming from the place of your inner heart and compass, not the mind. It's about being more connected and trusting your intuition and seeing yourself for who you are. Your intuition is the voice of the soul, and the soul is love. When you choose love, you have chosen to be open. You have chosen to look inside and see, "Fuck, I am magnificent."

Whatever is not love is fear. When you choose love, you accept everything for what and who it is. You are grateful. Love is gratitude, and gratitude takes what you have right now, every situation, event, failure, disability, and fault, and it glues the pieces of yourself back together. It even takes the parts that you have previously rejected so that you can see that you needed them to be whole.

Love is authenticity. It will give you the strength to reach up and remove the mask that you fear you cannot live without and know that you can no longer stand living within.

Love is awareness and acceptance of it all. Change starts within you. Love starts within you.

Start within, and you will feel and attract more love than you could have ever imagined. Trust in loving yourself. Forget the battle between your ears. *You are loveable.* There is no other bigger truth. Love is where you came from. It's what your spirit is built out of. The only distortion and argument is the noise that has built up over time in your mind. That noise is not real.

Lesson

45 | ENDINGS: Real Love Doesn't Have a Happily Ever After

The fear of abandonment can also be the fear of abandoning ourselves, but it is in the toughest moments that you find the strength to remain within yourself and that you find a way to reverse and dissolve the fear.

Remaining connected to what you feel, being present with what is happening, giving yourself the respect to process what you experience, and going easy on yourself for not being perfect are critical in minimizing your fears and scars. Listen, and feel.

Then act with honour and truth. Do what you know you must. This takes so much courage. It takes so much courage to change your perspective and change your direction. Know that when you are reacting, and know that when you need to stand for your worth.

Love is where true freedom lives, and no one can take love from you when you choose it.

We abandon ourselves by not listening to what we feel is right for our soul but believing what our mind tells us is right instead. Right now, you can decide not to abandon yourself. You can look inward, see your worth, and not allow the pain of another to slip from their lips and slice you to pieces. Your shield is self-love.

You are invincible when you know, embody, embrace, project, be, express and are love.

Know right now with complete and unwavering truth that you are worthy, simply because you exist.

When you stop abandoning you, you no longer fear losing anything because you realise that you are giving yourself everything that you need. Only then can you have healthy relationships with family, friends, and loved ones. Only then can you love and accept yourself and never withhold from yourself unconditional love.

Lesson

46 | HEALING: Love Collapses the Polarities and Heals Pain

No bullshit, love can heal everything. Love, when I write about it, is not the Romeo and Juliet kind of love. Remember when I explained the spinning top, the metaphor of consciousness at its highest frequency showing the spinning top as grey or wholeness and not as black and white or separateness? That was yin and yang making a whole.

The love that collapses polarities is a state of consciousness that has no time and space. It's completely undisrupted by any sense of polarity or binary. It's the state where things just are.

When we love something, I am saying that we accept it. We see its wholeness. We remove the emotional attachments and the resistance.

It has repeatedly been noted in scientific and medical texts how the miracles of transcending polarities and love can heal people's physical ailments. When you choose love, you can quite literally heal your life (Demartini).

Practically speaking, if we were to work through an event from the past for emotional healing, we would look at the imbalance in polarities causing the emotional pain.

Take the example of a father bullying his son. Typically, a person who blames their adult insecurities on a bully from their upbringing attracts more bullies. I find that these people have terrible boundaries of self-respect and self-love. They also often deny that they would ever have cruel characteristics of bullying within them; they deny that part of themselves. The practice of vulnerability and acceptance shows us that we all have every characteristic and trait within us, simply expressed in different ways. We have both negative and positive. It is through our love, our seeing of this—knowing the normality of this polarity of the human essence—that we are made emotionally stable and invincible.

Exercise: **Getting Real with Trauma**

When I coach someone through a past trauma, I help them by using these three steps:

1. Write down the very specific situation that you feel is responsible for your current problem or feeling. If it was a person rather than an event (for example: physical abuse as opposed to a house burning down), then list the action or name the characteristic of the person whom you feel is responsible.
2. If it's a person, begin to list the ways that you also express this same trait within yourself. If the trait is cruelty, list all of the ways throughout your life that you have been cruel to yourself, to others, and to the world until you are confident that you also express this trait. This requires incredible amounts of discipline, courage, and humility.
3. Next, list every benefit that has occurred as a direct or indirect result of this event. Dig deep, and think hard. It could take up to 100 benefits to balance the polarity of the judgment and negative aspects that you believe are causing your emotional pain.

Remember, it's not the event that causes the pain, it's our mentally limited perspective.

I want to clarify that this is not a justification process. This does not discredit the pain that you have experienced; it simply allows us to be free from that pain moving forward. So, release stored emotion, and end any cycles of attracting another similar event.

It is so important to be okay with falling apart. It is even more important to realise that to move through life, we are the ones responsible for picking ourselves back up again.

This exercise will help you transcend your thinking to a state of complete awareness where you can see the wholeness and not just the black darkness, which will put you in a disempowered negative state. It will allow you to see also the white light, the benefits. You will get to a point when you realise that despite the level of trauma that you or society labels the event, it was 100% necessary so you would never take it back.

This exercise is powerful not only in the sense that you begin to release old blame and emotional trauma but also because you begin to trust life when you see that absolutely everything that happens has no more or less black or white. It is always whole. It is only the ego's low vibration filter that sees anything in polarity.

Anytime that there is any form of judgment, resistance, or polarity there is ego. This is choosing fear. Choosing love simply means choosing to see the wholeness of what already is. It's a whole new level of understanding. We do not get what we want; we get what we need.

Your mind is so powerful. When you learn to weave love into your life and use it, your potential has no limit.

> *"You know you're in love when you can't fall asleep because reality is finally better than your dreams."*
>
> **—Dr. Seuss**

When you learn to choose love in every single moment, your life becomes a world of magic because you realise that there is magic everywhere. You see the miracles. You feel so alive and vibrant. You know in your core that no one can take it away from you.

Love is indestructible. Love is you.

Damn, how did I end up all cliché ;)

Lesson

47 | CHOOSE: Choosing Love is Choosing Freedom

When we choose love, we choose

- Empowerment
  We are no longer a victim of blame, guilt, or rage. We attract into our life empowerment, creativity, and inspiration. Love is the mind in a balanced state that results in a higher awareness. Love is a state of living, which is so incredibly conscious that no fear can penetrate it. We let go of the beliefs that hold us back in the past and define us as a physical form. When we let go of blame, we expand as a soul.

- Authenticity
  It allows us to become authentic in all we do.

- Freedom
  We are free. There is nothing except complete unapologetic, unconditional acceptance for all of us, the good, bad, and ugly.

- Power
  Our power becomes palpable, and we begin to experience our potential. The only opinion that matters is our own. When we become conscious and present, in flow, we realise that we aren't limited to the physical world. We live in it but aren't limited to it. We realise that what we say to ourselves is what will create our destiny, and we begin to realise that our world is the most important one of all.

- Choice
  We steer the ship, make the calls, and are more than happy to be accountable. We realise happiness is inside, and we stop searching for it outside of ourselves. Our future is ours, and with that power, we share our authentic selves through gratitude.

- Connection
  We are no longer alone, and we do not need anyone to make us feel complete. Our connection to the rest of the world becomes clear.

- Purpose
  Our purpose reveals itself to us through the haze of previous distraction. We have shown up, and we are ready.

- Community
  Everyone else becomes loveable as well. You let go of judgments; there are no rules. You embrace complete acceptance.

- Enough
  We understand that it's okay to screw up and embrace true vulnerability in our lives. We know love's essential role in personal freedom. No proof of our worth to another is required. We already know that we are enough.

- Creativity
  We understand fears dull creativity and truth. Life becomes worry-free. We are open and inspiring to others.

- Acceptance
  We accept all circumstances and events as our own creation and understand that love is always hidden at the bottom.

- Attraction
  We attract an equally self-worthy partner and breed harmony, generosity, and importance in all our relationships.

- Courage
  We realise courage is not the lack of fear, but the ability to accept any situation in its need to show us the lessons we need. Our worth is not based on outcomes, but through intention of everything we do.

- Light
  We are free to be ourselves. To shine into the world providing light and energy everywhere we go.

You made it! We are at the end. I am not only excited because I finished a fucking book but also because I now get to tell you the best bit *ever!*

You know all of those times that I told you to stop searching for happiness in sex, a packet of cookies, a Ferrari, a muscly rig, a wad of cash, Netflix, Prada heels, and all that jazz? Well, guess what? You can now enjoy the fuck out of those things.

The difference between consuming or indulging in the 7Fs pre and post unuckwithable is that pre unfuckwithable, you *needed them.* You craved them and consumed them through unconscious impulse. They were running your life. Post unfuckwithable, you enjoy them, love them, appreciate them, want them, and can freely taste them. You can then put them down just as easily as you picked them up.

Isn't that just the most divine news ever? Unfuckwithable isn't about never relishing in the external parts of life. Dammit, I fucking love beer; I love sex; I love watching the entire series of Star Wars in one weekend, and I am definitely going to own a pair of red sole Louboutin heels before I die. I am not suggesting that you to go without these things. I am trying to teach you how to enjoy them in a way that is free.

In Summary

Want the honest unfuckwithable?

Simple version:

> *"Fear is the path to the dark side."*

> **—Yoda**

Don't follow your fearful thoughts. Don't do it, okay?

Choose you, choose light, choose life.

It's all going to work out if you always remember that it begins and ends with you.

Start on the shit that you hate about yourself. See if you can let one little thing go each week. Then, move to the people who you hate. Start to see yourself in them. Be cool with them, and be cool with you.

Complex version:

Dig into your past, your monsters, and your cobwebs. Peek in, and realise that love can fix it. Your brain has judged something, and now, you want to throw things at your mother/brother/best friend/lover, but you know that you shouldn't.

Maybe, you could just stop giving a shit. That would help. I believe that would really, really help right now.

My car broke down; I don't give a shit.

I put on three kilograms, and my cellulite has gone from mid-arse to mid-thigh. Who gives a shit?

My girlfriend cheated on me, zero shits were given.

My dad never calls me on my birthday, and he's a hypocritical douche-bag. I do not give a shit.

Now, just look at all that new energy you have. We do stuff, some of it feels good, and some of it doesn't. We are all just here trying to figure it out.

Please, stop giving a shit about things that wouldn't matter to you on your death bed.

Let it go.

Surrender.

Be okay with life.

Be okay with yourself.

Smell some flowers.

Get drunk.

Have dirty sex.

Read *Harry Potter* at the age of 32 and not care.

Fall in love.

Get out of your comfort zone.

Figure out who you are after 47 tequilas.

Don't die from alcohol poisoning.

Wear sparkly clothes.

Buy stupidly expensive and uncomfortable heels because they are sexy as fuck.

And then, realise that all you ever needed is already yours.

It's inevitable; with or without my help, you are going to break down at some point and realise that you don't like some of the stuff that you've been doing. And then, you will change it.

Just don't get too lost in the change bit. That's all I hope to do, ease the blow when you realise that you could have stopped living a life that you didn't love. But remember, what you did was what you did. It's what you needed to do.

Stop sweating about whether you have made it or woken up.

You will get there all in good time.

Explore this crazy world. Have an adventure with life.

Go figure out what unfuckwithable is for you.

I urge you to head out on a treasure hunt for the parts of yourself that you've placed in a box and labelled wrong. Open the box and love the fuck out of them.

And then, *start to take up space,*

in a loving, open, kind, and fearless way.

There is so much space for us all to fit. Stop shrinking into half of yourself, thinking that showing the perfect parts makes you strong.

No, it only weakens you and cripples you at a soul level.

You'll realise that the broken bits that you were trying to hide were the exact thing that you were looking for to make you whole.

It feels normal for me to be curious about people doing things differently, not different and famous, just different and real. These people tend to push the status quo with their existence. Unafraid to show up and take up space. These people show us how, by doing so, we inspire the letting go of the ego and judgment and shame. Because when you are hiding a part of yourself, only showing up a little, not shaking cages and rattling hearts, you are creating a deep shame within, a belief that part of you is wrong. So, you hide. Silence grows shame.

Be loud in your wholeness.

Shine.

After all, everything is a choice, so make the decision now to spend the rest of your life doing what you truly give a fuck about.

There will be stuff that you don't want to do, like taxes, visiting your great-nan who smells funny, and being nice to your mother-in-law. Deal with it. Do it with love.

Once you learn the simple fact that you'll always eventually get to where you need to go, you'll let go of searching.

Relax.

Let life be.

And you're really, *really* going to be okay.

All that remains is to leave you with a few lines from possibly the most profound piece of reading that I have ever come across. It is the closest representation of the unfuckwithable philosophy that you'll find outside of this book...

Love,

Ambz

You have brains in your head.
You have feet in your shoes.
You can steer yourself any direction you choose.

And remember that life's a great balancing act.

Kid, you'll move mountains!

You're off to Great Places!
Today is your day!

—Excerpts from
Oh the Places You'll Go!
by Dr. Seuss

REFERENCES

Clinical Depression.co.uk. Major Depression Facts. N.p., 2013. Web. 17 July 2016.

Demartini, J. 'The Mind Body Connection', *Writings and Insights Written, Audio and Video from Dr. Demartini*. Accessed 10 October 2015.

Eckhart Tolle: Living Your True Purpose. 2012. video. Sarno, J E. *The Divided Mind*. New York: Regan Books, 2006.

Health at A Glance 2015. 8th ed. Paris: OECD Publishing, 2015. Print.

Latin Definition for: Addico, Addicere, Addixi, Addictus. *Oxford Latin Dictionary* 1982. Web. 17 July 2016.

Shantall, Dr. T. 'Meaninglessness and Suicidal Risk', *Logotherapy World Congress 2011*. Accessed 14 September 2015.

Prabhune, Akanksha. "10 Inspirational & Successful People Who Did Not Let Failure Define Them". *Storypick*. N.p., 2017. Web. 17 Mar. 2017.

"The Likely Cause Of Addiction Has Been Discovered, And It Is Not What You Think". *The Huffington Post*. N.p., 2017. Web. 17 Mar. 2017.

Hari, Johann. *Chasing The Scream*. 1st ed. New York: Blooms-bury, 2016. Print.

Sarno, John E. *The Divided Mind*. 1st ed. New York: Harper Col-lins, 2007. Print.

Vogler, Christopher. *A Practical Guide To Joseph Cambell's The Hero With A Thousand Faces*. 1985. Web. 28 Mar. 2017.

ABOUT THE AUTHOR

Amber is an Australian country gal with a big, bold, and audacious heart. A Diploma of Mindfulness based Cognitive Behavioural Therapy, a qualified Neuro-Linguistic Programming Practitioner, and a Deep State Re-Patterning Therapist are some of the professional qualifications and tools that Amber brings to her work around emotional, mental, and spiritual self-mastery.

Amber's previous work in western medicine, with a Bachelor of Medical Radiation Science: Radiation Therapy, eventually steered her study both personally and professionally towards, neuroscience, human behaviour, mind-body connection, and spiritual philosophy. Amber brings both practicality and an open, rational, and well-rounded perspective to everything that she does.

Amber uses what may seem like counter intuitive approach to self-help. She is mischievously antagonistic and facetious as a speaker, writer, and mentor, dedicated to helping people find what it is that they stand for within themselves and in life. Amber has been single-handedly running her own company of retreats, live events, one on one coaching, and online programs for half a decade. Amber's education, work, and relationships contribute to the genuine wisdom and expertise in everything that she teaches.

CPSIA information can be obtained
at www.ICGtesting.com
Printed in the USA
LVHW051405030520
654907LV00004B/1408